Contents

Contents

Contents

Chapter One

Religious Dialogue and the Future of Theology

The New State of Theology

Postmodernity and the Crisis in Catholic Theology

In recent years, some Catholic theologians who were previously regarded as mainstream thinkers have been simultaneously praised and reviled by various colleagues, church officials, and commentators in the Catholic media. Take, for example, the publications of Jacques Dupuis's *Toward a Christian Theology of Religious Pluralism* and Roger Haight's *Jesus Symbol of God.*[1] Both authors won the Catholic Press Association Book Award for the best theology book of the year for these books, and both authors found themselves being investigated by the Vatican's Congregation of the Doctrine of the Faith (CDF) for these very same texts. Why the uproar? In a postmodern context, these authors, and many like them, have suggested that the very nature of Catholic theology must take into account the truth claims of other religious traditions.

Theological pluralism has been a fact throughout the whole life of the church, and consciously so since the nineteenth century, with the writings of such revered thinkers as John Henry Newman and Maurice Blondel. In more recent times, the bishops of Vatican II insisted upon it when they rejected the scholastic dominance represented by the Theological Commission and Cardinal Ottoviani of the Holy Office (now CDF). The fathers of

Vatican II opted for and modeled a broader pluralistic theological approach brought on by such giants as Jean Daneleou, Henri de Lubac, Hans Urs von Balthasar, Edward Schillebeeckx, and Karl Rahner. One only has to remember how dramatic were those days. For example, Cardinal Ottoviani placed Rahner on his list barring him from even being present in the city of Rome during the sessions of Vatican II. Pope Paul VI not only rejected this political (theological?) move, but made Rahner one of the council's formal theological experts (a *peritus*). In fact, Rahner is widely regarded as having been the chief architect of Vatican II's Dogmatic Constitution on the Church *(Lumen Gentium)*. Rahner and many others represented a clear change toward a new theological worldview.

The theological climate has changed even more dramatically in the past forty years. In the 1960s, Cardinal Ottoviani asked other bishops of Vatican II point blank, "Are these fathers planning a revolution?"[2] Their theological approach was simply one he could not comprehend. Now, at the beginning of the twenty-first century, his successor Cardinal Ratzinger is asking if there is yet another revolution, one the CDF has resisted.[3] Today, instead of advancing the very challenging notion of *theological* pluralism, many theologians are acknowledging a *religious* pluralism. They are self-consciously theologizing in light of the presence of other religious traditions, taking into account religious claims beyond Christian revelation. Many are even asking about the very nature of religious truth claims and their necessary limitations, and are providing new analyses as to how religious truth works in the first place.[4]

One wonders if Pope John Paul II hadn't actually modeled this. In describing his Assisi Day of Prayer in 1987 to the Cardinals of the Curia and in a later speech he gave in India, he asserted that there are insights in other religions that have been revealed by God that have not been revealed to Christianity.[5] The fact that this global village of ours has other religions or religious insights is hardly news. That we ought to consider them and their truth claims *while* doing Catholic theology is indeed nothing short of a revolution.

A few years ago I spoke on a panel about Vatican II that included James Shannon, who participated at the council. When asked about the most far-reaching document of the whole council, Shannon suggested that it was the Pastoral Constitution of the Church in the Modern World *(Gaudium et Spes)*. A fellow panelist then spoke up: "What we need now," he said, "is a Constitution of the Church in the *Postmodern* World." Things have changed. So what does it mean to live in *postmodernity*? First, it means that we live in an age of heightened historical consciousness. We are now particularly sensitive to the fact that all human ideas and expressions are rooted in a unique historical place and time. No articulation of truth, therefore, is exempt from historical or philosophical critique. Second, we are suspicious of a *classisist* notion of knowing or of having privileged access to truth. Particularly hard hit is the Enlightenment assumption that truth can be extricated from cultural assumptions, especially when the Enlightenment itself is a dominating Western European interpretation of culture. What were previously understood as objective interpretations of truth are now exposed as expressions of Western domination and paternalism. We must, it is argued, take the other as truly other, as a very different version of reality. In essence, we have come to a greater appreciation of the relativity of our own perspectives.[6] Roger Haight says it well: "The sheer age and size of reality compounds our sense of relativity."[7]

We live in a cultural and religious world where universal truth claims themselves are either challenged or at least required to be put into a context that is skeptical of universals and wary of top-down dogmas. In the place of abstract and highly philosophical presentations of the faith, our postmodern landscape must now appeal to the plurality of experience. And it needs to be done in the context in which we live, that is, in a religiously plural environment. In sum, we desperately need to be dialogue with those around us.

The Critical Move toward the Other

Already in the early 1960s, Paul Tillich called interreligious dialogue the greatest modern theological challenge and the distinctive journey of our time.[8] David Tracy agrees: "There is no more difficult or more pressing question on the present theological horizon than that of interreligious dialogue."[9] Some, myself included, have argued that not only is dialogue essential for an understanding of and common respect for others, but that it can even help a Christian become a better Christian. We look at another closely and we see things about the religious quest and the human spirit differently. There is a saying: "When you learn a different language you learn a new way of thinking." This is what dialogue does. Among other things, it helps us learn a new way of thinking about the spiritual journey.

Too often quick judgments are made in comparative religion. Some are readily dismissive of others. Despite John Paul II's declaration of the possibility of a plurality of revelations, he had unfairly dismissed Buddhism as a religion seeking to escape the world.[10] While some Buddhist language arguably supports this, as would some Christian language, it is superficial and misleading. Likewise, Hans Urs von Balthasar distinguished Christian contemplation from Eastern meditations by asserting that the Christian form is supernatural and based on love, while Eastern forms are natural and ultimately narcissistic.[11] Had von Balthasar actually studied any of them carefully? All of them?

On the other hand, it is far more common to find approaches with quite different conclusions. Far more prevalent, for example, are philosophers and theologians who have argued that Allah, Trinity, Yahweh, Krishna, Brahman, Nirvana, Tao, and so on, all name the same transcendental reality. Given that God is beyond all conception and each conception is limited anyway, it matters little what we call God; each term refers to the same reality.[12]

This *perennialism* takes on many different forms. While some claim that all religions bear witness to the same ultimate reality, others, from Carl Jung to Rudolph Otto, assert that all religions have the same psychic origins and deal with the same psychic content.[13] Still others have argued that the underlying experience in all religions is the same. More than a century ago William James wrote, "When we survey the whole field of religion, we find a great variety in the thoughts of those who have prevailed there; but the feelings [mystical intuitions] on the one hand, and the content on the other are almost always the same, for the Stoic, Christian, and Buddhist saints are practically indistinguishable in their lives."[14] Still further, some have asserted that conceptions of God do matter and drastically differ, but what is the same is the project of salvation. Every religion is, in effect, a different path to top of the same mountain.[15]

To these assertions and many like them we could also ask: How do you know? How can one, at the start, determine that various spiritualities are either fundamentally the same or radically different? In fact, while many readers would find Balthasar's all-too-easy distinction disturbing and even arrogant, is it less arrogant to simply equate them all? Wouldn't it be insulting to a Buddhist if a Christian said, "I know all about *Nirvana*; this is what we mean by God" (or heaven, or kingdom of God, take your pick). Robert Florida reports of a Zen Master stating that he never felt so far from Zen as when a Christian was describing it.[16] I find it disturbing that so many of these influential thinkers can feel free to make such broad claims across the board: they are ultimately all the same, they ultimately all have the same God, or they ultimately all experience the same thing. Can we really equate on any of these levels all religions—Native American Shamanism with Buddhism, with Christianity, with Shintoism, with Hindu Vedanta, with Haitian Voodoo?

One example may suffice. A central tenet for many Hindus is the belief that the inner self *(atman)* ought to be identified (in various ways) to ultimate reality *(Brahman)*. This insight is key to the soul's liberation. The Buddha, on the other hand, taught that the very belief in an *atman* prohibits one from liberation. Which is it? Are they complementary truths? Could they both be true and synthesized on some transcendent level? How could one equate the Hindu experience of the *atman*'s union and identification with *Brahman* to the Buddhist experience of *Nirvana*, which is the clearest rejection that there even is an *atman*? Maybe it is indeed possible to show how they can be integrated, perhaps as a paradoxical synthesis. But to suggest from the start that this is the case doesn't take seriously the very real differences among religions. This seemingly openhanded desire to sympathize with other religions actually has the tendency to dismiss their fundamental reason for being.

What we see is that there is a great need to actually engage the other before we come to any assessments. But far more than simply judgment about the other can be reaped through interreligious dialogue. This *more* is principally what this book intends to explore. This small volume intends not at all to add to the many articles and books on religious pluralism, its methods, problems, and possibilities. Rather this book is an attempt at a kind of dialogue. My "dialogue partners" are two classical representatives of the Christian and Buddhist traditions, Saint John of the Cross and Bhadantacariya Buddhaghosa. While these two representatives cannot speak for the whole of either the Christian or the Theravada Buddhist tradition, they do represent themes, practices, and theological commitments that are broadly agreed upon in their respective spiritual traditions. John of the Cross was not so much an innovator of the contemplative journey to God as he was a systematizer of a long, venerable tradition.[17] Likewise, Buddhaghosa holds an extraordinary position in the Theravada tradition. In preparing for this book I have read some thirty books on Buddhist meditation. In every presentation, the author cites Buddhaghosa directly as either the only source or the primary source.[18]

What I propose is that we study three central themes in the Christian and Buddhist spiritual life, namely, the human being (*Who* are we?), the path of the spiritual life (*How* do we become holy?), and the descriptions of their respective ultimate horizons, that is, union with God and *Nirvana* (*What* are we striving for?). We shall see that there are extraordinary convergences in the theologies and spiritualities of these two revered saints and theologians. But there are also divergences that suggest they are in many ways operating in very different spiritual universes. I am proposing here a model for how interreligious dialogue can proceed. This book is not revolutionary, but it does reflect the new world we are already living in. But first we should lay a little groundwork on the nature of dialogue and our assumptions going in.

Interreligious Dialogue

Why Dialogue at All?

If a Christian believes that Jesus Christ is the "Way, the Truth, and the Life" (John 14:5), the "expression and full image of God" (Heb 1:3; Col 1:15), and indeed the head and Lord of all things in the heaven and earth (Eph 1:10; Phil 2:10–11), then what good could a Christian possibly get from dialogue with others outside of the Christian revelation? What would we hope to learn from others? It may be interesting to listen to others' views and practices, but what does it actually achieve beyond satisfying one's curiosity? The specific goals of dialogue are addressed in the following pages, but I believe that dialogue expands one's heart, mind, and soul in ways that nothing else can. Being in dialogue with Hindus and Buddhists has even helped me understand my Christian faith better. For example, I have long believed that Christ teaches a way of self-offering, a dying to the old self in love, that a new Christlike self might emerge. Our tradition is replete with exhortations to this kind of self-offering. Likewise, Saint Paul's writings are filled with descriptions of this new life in the Spirit. But I must confess that it was in reading the Hindu classic, *Bhagavad Gita*, that I understood this profound expression of self-donation in a wholly new and radical way. In the *Gita*, using various examples, lessons, and images,

God as Krishna teaches the hero Arjuna to perform his religious and temporal duties *(dharma)* in a pure way. This is challenging enough, but Krishna goes further. Arjuna is then admonished to refuse to identify with his virtue or with the merit *(karma)* that this produces. Rather, Arjuna ought to offer this *karma* as a loving gift to him. One leaves the *Gita* with the mantra, "Perform your *dharma*, renounce the fruit of your *karma*." What I saw was not only a very close description of dying to oneself, but also a profound expression of detaching from oneself all things, so that, as Saint Paul says, "God may be all in all" (1 Cor 15:28).

What I saw was a truth I already believed in a new way. I realized that, even when I was doing good ministry and was lovingly present to others, I was identifying with that ministry. There was this big, unconscious "I" that was involved. *I'm* extending myself to this other person; *I'm* trying to be generous; *I'm* trying to be virtuous. But if I offer all that I am and do as an act of love for Jesus Christ, then I shouldn't claim anything. This letting go of the big *I*, something I learned from the *Gita*, has been very freeing for me as a minister. In short, the *Gita* helped me understand something very Christian, and in a way I had not anticipated. Later I was reading Saint Thérèse of Lisieux's *The Story of a Soul*. Her famous "little way" expresses a life of offering everything she did and was to God as a sacrifice of love. It was from reading of the *Gita* that I understood Thérèse more profoundly.

I also remember a profound Tibetan Buddhist liturgy that I participated in as part of a Buddhist-Christian dialogue. The Tibetan monks were seeking to take in the energy of violence and hatred in the world—taking to themselves the "bad *karma*" of others—so that the monks might relieve the world of the weight of evil and transform this negative energy into love. They were identifying with and taking onto themselves the sins of the world. In a radical way, this is what Jesus did for humanity. I took from that profound liturgy a renewed challenge to act as a sacrament of Christ in striving to do the same. I don't believe in *karma* in the same way that Buddhists do, and I couldn't completely enter this liturgy as a Christian in the way that the monks were performing it. But by taking part in this Buddhist liturgy, on some level I saw my Christian path in a new light.

There is also something about articulating what one believes, and listening to another *as* other that simply changes the listener. V. P. Vineeth once wrote, "Man is dialogical by nature. He communicates himself to others by self-awareness and is transformed in that communication."[19] There is something about the human spirit that needs to share in order to actually understand oneself.

There is, further, a moral imperative to dialogue. Many theologians believe that dialogue ought to precede the Christian missionary commandment to "go and make disciples of all nations" (Matt 28:19), not only in procedure, but also in priority. That is, not only is it critical to understand those to whom one witnesses, but understanding and mutual respect are of a higher imperative. You cannot love your neighbors if you are not engaged with them. You cannot love them if you do not honor their sincere religious claims of experience. And authentic engagement requires not seeing them only as potential candidates for conversion, but as truly and fully human, deserving of respect for the gifts and insights that they already have.

This last reason for dialogue also brings to the table the issue of credibility. When a Buddhist believes that a Christian is speaking to him only in order to convert him, that Christian loses credibility. The Buddhist can rightly ask: How can you say you love me, if you don't know me? How can you say you care about me when you are uninterested in who I am and what I believe? You wish me to be open to your message, but do you have this same essential openness? Dialogue doesn't suppress or replace missionary activity, but it ought to precede it.

One never knows what can happen in an encounter with another. In fact, one may learn something from another that one can incorporate in one's own spiritual life. This isn't an attempt at a hybrid religious life, as if I can take a little from one religion that

I like, a little from another, and a little from my home base. Religious syncretism makes one little more than a spiritual dilettante, and I am convinced that it is a philosophically and logically misplaced effort. In a word, it lacks coherency. But one never knows how one is going to be affected. For example, I argue at the end of this book that there are Buddhist meditation techniques that a Christian can practice that not only do not weaken one's Christian faith, but actually converge with the very theology that is part of our tradition.

The Posture for Dialogue

Having reviewed stacks of literature about interreligious dialogue, I have gleaned a fairly consistent, universally agreed-upon list of conditions and intentions for authentic dialogue. The first condition is that it should be *without any ulterior or covert motives.* In the past, the motive for dialogue has often been either for conversion or to provide a forum for one or both partners to demonstrate the superiority of their own positions. Vineeth again: "One cannot presuppose error as a condition of dialogue."[20]

Second, one must come to the table with *essential openness.* Such openness refers to trying to understand not only what the partner says conceptually, but also what the other means and the reality the other is trying to convey. Because religious language is used differently in various traditions, this kind of openness requires both an intellectual availability to new ideas and theological paradigms as well as an intuitive openness to the deep truth the other is trying to communicate. Another level of openness is the ability to critically reassess one's own tradition. I must be free enough to truly be challenged. And finally, one has to be open to the process. This means not trying to predict or manipulate the dialogue experience. Perhaps it will be at times disagreeable. So be it. If I enter into a dialogue with another with the preconception that everything the other says that does not correspond to what I believe is wrong, this undermines the experience. In the same vein, if I enter into it with some need to accept anything and everything offered as if it were necessarily true, my openness is in the end dubious.

Third, it is imperative that other religious traditions are *respected in their own right* and on their own terms. This is perhaps one of the central imperatives of interreligious dialogue: that traditions are taken seriously for what they are in themselves. This means, for example, not just regarding another faith as simply one of many manifestations of some common spiritual or mystical essence. Respecting other traditions in their own right also means being able to understand them and reiterate their central beliefs, practices, and spiritual ethos in a way that they themselves would recognize and agree with.

Fourth, in the spirit of trust and openness, *differences are not to be eschewed.* Rather, they can even be highlighted. If we do not exploit differences between us, we can appreciate their power to challenge us to rethink our own assumptions. In some past experiences of dialogue, there seemed to be a covert need for some kind of uniformity or of approaching all religious ways as equally valid or essentially the same. This resulted in a contrived effort for respect. It is the exploration of differences between religious worlds that allows one to criticize and renew one's awareness of one's own tradition.[21] Indeed, similarities discovered can teach us much about what may be universal to authentic religious paths. However, avoiding differences or playing them down is a tragic and often practiced mistake. One could ask the question simply: If there's nothing much different about us, why dialogue at all? It is often the differences that make the very dialogue fruitful.

The fifth and final criterion for good dialogue is more of a caveat: *Make no hasty determinations* about the other, and keep in check the need to overgeneralize or categorize the religious life of the other. We must realize that we know and can legitimately say less than we might want to about the other. Interreligious dialogue is holy ground with much mystery, and we should walk barefoot and humbly.

Goals and Possibilities in Dialogue

Virtually everyone agrees that dialogue can become a great *forum for personal growth* and transformation. John Cobb writes, "To hear another articulation of a truth is to be changed by that truth."[22] And no matter how one assesses whether or not that articulation should be appropriated, Cobb echoes a universalized point of view. It changes one to be engaged with another, particularly if that other brings a whole new spiritual perspective and practice.

Another goal is that it could raise a *critique to one's own religious life*. To remain enclosed in one's own tradition provides a danger of not seeing how it looks from the outside. Its assumptions are never called into question. How, for example, would Americans look at our foreign policy if we regularly spoke to Europeans, Asians, Africans, and Latin Americans about politics? Surely such discussions would make us reassess our own policies in a very different light. By suggesting the possibility of critique, I am not thinking of a wholesale rejection of one's tradition. Instead, one might discover a distortion of one's own belief, or an overdeveloped part of the tradition might be balanced by an alternative voice.

Third, dialogue can actually *strengthen one's own spiritual tradition*. It can lay bare one's assumptions, usually unconsciously held, and force one to a better, more clearly grounded conviction of what one holds true. One could, for example, see Christ differently and his relevance to one's life even more fully by encounter with another. We can reexperience Christian convictions in light of the contrast that they may have with the other. I was in a Buddhist-Christian dialogue some years ago, and one of the Buddhist representatives remarked at how every room in the monastery had a crucifix. He wanted to discuss this. I had been so used to them that they didn't even register. Sometimes we can domesticate our deepest symbols, and it takes an outside voice to highlight their prominence.

A fourth goal for dialogue is that it can *expand one's horizons of awareness*. We see things from a different point of view, and we can get an expanded sense of broader human transcendental experience. It may also be that there are insights from another's religious tradition that could actually complement deficiencies in one's own faith, even as they strengthen one's own religious tradition. Shortly before he died, Thomas Merton wrote that for some Christian monastics, learning a religious discipline from another tradition could not only assist a given monk, but also contribute to monastic renewal in the Western church.[23]

Last Note: Dialogue and Spiritual Practice

Some scholars involved in interreligious dialogue have found that previous attempts at dialogue, while contributing many important insights, have proven to be lacking in that they have not included interreligious practice. It is argued that one cannot even understand the theologies of others without some sense of the experience that their religious language and categories intend to convey.[24] Augustine Morris puts it this way: "Teaching Buddhism without meditation is like teaching swimming without water."[25] Abhishiktananda (Father Henri Le Saux), a pioneer in Hindu-Christian dialogue, has argued that the real purpose of dialogue is to understand the religious *experience* of the other, and that this can never come from intellectual discussions alone. "Dialogue," he said, "should be *sadhana* or spiritual praxis."[26]

In fact, this kind of interreligious dialogue is already happening. Ordinary lay people as well as official representatives of various religious professions are already engaged in practicing forms of religious devotion outside of their home traditions.[27] In terms of method, this is the most complex issue in dialogue, and that which has been given the least critical reflection.[28] Questions have been raised about whether or not interreligious practice is even possible without proposing a spirituality that lacks coherency. We must not easily dismiss the poignant question of whether or not non-Christian techniques can be extracted from spiritual goals that are in conflict with the gospel. As a Christian, can I really worship Krishna? We must also not fail to take seriously the issue as to *how* such techniques can be used. The last chapter of this volume deals with the question of interreligious practice.

Our Dialogue Partners: John of the Cross and Buddhaghosa

Saint John of the Cross

Before we engage in a kind of dialogue with the texts written by Saint John and Buddhaghosa, perhaps a brief word is in order about who they are. Saint John of the Cross is considered in the Roman Catholic tradition as one of the greatest expositors of the contemplative, mystical path to union with God. While no one can claim an exclusive voice in the tradition, he perhaps more than any other holds preeminence. In 1542, Juan de Yepes was born in a small Castilian town of Fontiveros. As a child, and after his father had died, his family moved to Medino del Campo, where he entered a school for the poor and received his primary education. At seventeen, he was enrolled at a Jesuit school of higher education for four years. The foundation of this schooling was philosophy and humanities. In 1563, when John was twenty-one years old, he entered the Carmelite Order, and in 1564 he began formal studies at the University of Salamanca.[29]

Even as a student, John's life of asceticism was apparent. He was attested to have been devoted, when not attending lectures, to sitting at his desk engrossed in his academic work, while he spent large parts of every night in prayer. He was reported as having fasted assiduously and practiced bodily mortifications.

After leaving the university, and during the twenty-three years of work in the newly reformed Carmelite order, he was assigned numerous, highly responsible positions. He held offices as novice master, student master, prior, spiritual director, rector, provincial, and counselor to the vicar general. Thus, in the man who would teach what appears to be a highly individualistic journey of the soul to God, we find a life that was filled with numerous and often high-profile pastoral duties.

To situate John's writings within the framework of his life, it is important to understand how people experienced him as well as how he related to others. John was known for his humor, gentleness, and joy.[30] He enjoyed many personal friendships, and his extant letters are filled with warmth, compassion, and love. Part of John's spirituality that is not found in his writings was his liturgical piety.[31] This is important to note, since it is easy for one to read his contemplative path as suggesting that all meditative or sacramental piety must be relinquished as one progresses. Actually, he incorporated a sacramental piety with his contemplative life. He was also very interested in nature and art. Certainly in poetics he is regarded as a great Spanish figure. In addition, he had a visually artistic eye. He often spent time cultivating gardens and decorating chapels as well as creating his own paintings and carvings.

A superficial reading of his works, especially in terms of his more dramatic teachings on detachment and *leaving the world*, gives many readers the impression that he was dualistic, or that he regarded all forms of sensory joy suspiciously. Arguably, there is language that seems to support this.[32] Therefore, interpretation of his writings requires an attention to the facts of his life. He was surely an austere man, ascetical in many ways, and he was rigorous in his approach to the spiritual life. But he was also a gentle man, a man who loved the world generously and enjoyed it liberally.

Buddhism and Buddhaghosa

Christians place Saint John of the Cross in a religious context of which we are relatively familiar. The same cannot be said of Buddhaghosa's Buddhism. So before we look at the biography of this fifth-century giant, it may do us some good to understand Buddhism in general.

Hindu Background

The Hindu religious context, in which the Buddha experienced his own liberation and taught the practices leading toward it, was complex. There is no Hinduism exactly, at least not one that represents all Hindus. We might be better served to say that there is a Hindu religious tradition with some general cosmological and soteriological agreement. What I describe here represents Hinduism in very broad strokes. From earliest expressions of Hinduism (Rig Vedas c. 1200–1000 BCE) to its most developed form, represented by the Upanishads (c. 800–300 BCE), the universe was understood to be structured in terms of cause and effect.[33] This was the law of *karma*. Some of the Vedas, particularly texts known as the Brahmanas, describe the primary spiritual agenda as engaging the laws of *karma* for one's direct benefit. This was mostly through ritual action. For example, if one needed the gods to act beneficently, one performed a particular religious rite that obligated the gods to give the boon. Cause and effect was the underlying framework. In later Vedic texts, the same law of cause and effect was progressively understood as capable of manipulation for a better rebirth. No longer did this occur through ritual efficacy alone, but more important, through moral efficacy. One's reincarnation and the *karma* that produced it were understood to be primarily effected by one's life of virtue and inner wisdom. The possibility of gaining an excellent rebirth thus became a central interest.[34]

In the Upanishads, one sees a developing shift in spiritual preoccupation. The belief in reincarnation due to the law of cause and effect was not challenged, but the ultimate value of rebirth itself was. There arose interest no longer in manipulating rebirth through *karmic* law, but rather in escaping it altogether. Now for the spiritual virtuoso, spiritual practices led to the unmoving center of the wheel of *samsara* (literally "wandering"—from one life to another). The world was understood as ultimately dissatisfying and in this sense illusory. The great religious quest, therefore, was to escape *(moksha)* the illusory world and to enter into that which is absolute and ultimate.

The only reality that was not considered transient and ultimately illusory was the *atman*, the inner, ultimate self (soul). Depending upon one's interpretation, this self was a portion of or the essence of *Brahman*, the uncaused ultimate. Some Upanishads appear to even identify the *atman* with *Brahman* itself. *Brahman* is what we might legitimately call God. Much of Hindu Upanishadic thought is rooted in the conviction that everything has an *atman* and that "*atman* is *Brahman*." The transcendent essence of all that is, particularly one's inner self is that of the universal divine Brahman. To know *atman* as *Brahman* required great asceticism and meditation.

Buddha's Response

The Buddha (c. 563–480 BCE) did not reject the general Upanishadic tradition, which sought release by a higher knowledge attained through meditation. On the contrary, he wholeheartedly embraced it. He did, however, diverge from his Hindu tradition in three decided ways: in fundamental anthropology, in the nature of liberation, and in the types of meditation needed for liberation. According to the Buddha, wrong views and wrong practices not only do not destroy, but they can even serve to strengthen *samsaric* bondage.[35]

From his own experiences the Buddha taught several religious fundamentals that follow these three divergences. These are still regarded today as foundational by Buddhists of traditions as diverse as Zen, Tibetan, and Theravadin. They include the Four Noble Truths, a new view of the nature of all things (especially the human being), and the necessary mental training that brings *moksha*, which Buddha referred to as *Nirvana*.[36]

Here briefly are sketched the Buddha's Four Noble Truths. The First Noble Truth is that life is *dukkha*, which was a claim that nearly everyone in Buddha's religious culture already believed. *Dukkha* is often translated as "suffering," yet this does not convey its subtlety, which is more like "dissatisfaction." It refers to everything, even pleasure, as not fully satisfying to the soul. The Second Noble Truth is that the cause of *dukkha* is thirst or desire *(tanha)*. Thirst is the central cause of suffering in this life and the cause of rebirths to future lives. Not having something that we want is painful, but so is getting it and seeing that it fails to satisfy the thirst. One's *dukkha* in life is directly proportional to one's thirst or desire. The Third Noble Truth is simply that there exists the possibility of freedom from *dukkha*. And the Fourth Noble Truth: *Nirvana* represents this liberation.

Given the Fourth Noble Truths, the path leading to the cessation of suffering is the Buddha's Eightfold Path of (1) right understanding, (2) right thought, (3) right speech, (4) right action, (5) right livelihood, (6) right effort, (7) right mindfulness, and (8) right concentration. These eight, cultivated together, provide the spiritual aspirant with the context to realize *Nirvana*. Right speech, action, and livelihood represent the moral foundations of Buddhism. Right effort, mindfulness, and concentration converge as the meditative aspect of Buddhist spiritual development. They represent how the mind is trained, disciplined, and developed. The first two aspects of the Eightfold Path constitute the wisdom necessary for enlightenment. Right thought involves thoughts of selfless renunciation or detachment. And Right understanding involves both the act of seeing reality as it is and the *way* in which one looks at reality, particularly in spiritual practice.

Many of Buddha's discourses focus on the nature of reality and the importance of seeing this nature clearly. All reality (except *Nirvana*) has the same fundamental characteristics: *impermanence* (everything changes), *selflessness* (there is no concrete identity), and *dissatisfaction* (nothing ultimately satisfies). Right understanding views these characteristics by direct experience.

Bhadantacariya Buddhaghosa

Almost nothing is known with historical certainty about Buddhaghosa.[37] Apart from having an impressive compilation of his commentaries, all we really know is that he wrote in Sri Lanka in the early part of the fifth century CE. The most important source concerning Buddhaghosa is a Ceylonese historical chronicle, the *Mahavamsa*, the thirty-seventh chapter being devoted to him. Some of the historical reliability of the *Mahavamsa* is currently regarded as questionable. What is beyond dispute is that Buddhaghosa lived and wrote for some time in the monastery of Anaradhapura in the fifth century, that he wrote numerous commentaries on the Buddhist teachings there, including his classic text, *The Path of Purification*, and that his influence spread from Sri Lanka to other parts of Southeast Asia, especially Burma, shortly after his death.

There are two predominant legendary sources concerning his life. One comes from the *Mahavamsa*, and the other comes from Burmese hagiography (stories of saints). That they are based on scant facts about Buddhaghosa and appear largely mythological should not prevent us from deriving insight from them. According to the *Mahavamsa*, Buddhaghosa was an Indian Brahmin (elite caste) who was as precocious as he was brilliant. At an early age he was a public debater of religious truth, and as a young man he came upon a Buddhist monk who asked him the meaning of a particular spiritual teaching. Not able to answer, he begged to come to higher insight. His questioner told him that if he were to properly understand such sublime truth, he must convert to the Buddhist faith and enter the monastic order. It was only there that insight into the truth could be gained.

Some time after Buddhaghosa's conversion, the *Mahavamsa* says that he traveled to Sri Lanka, as the monastery of Anaradhapura was then the center of orthodoxy and the site of the greatest collection of Buddhist canonical texts. His initial interest was in translating the Sinhalese texts into Pali, that is, from the Sri Lankan to the Indian language. But the monks overseeing the texts wished to test him to determine whether he was worthy of such a charge. He was given a riddle to solve: *How does one untangle the tangle with which one is entangled?* If his solution proved adequate, he would be allowed to proceed with his task of translating the canon and commentaries.

The massive *Path of Purification* represents the answer to that riddle, which, legend goes, he wrote in one sitting. In order to demonstrate his wisdom, a *deva* (quasi-god) made his commentary invisible before he was able to show his examiners. This forced him to write it again. But this *deva* made the second copy invisible as well, thus forcing a third copy. When he presented this third copy to his examiners, the *deva* then made the other two copies visible. Upon reading all three, his examiners found them to be identical to the letter. This became proof that his answer was divinely inspired.

In the Burmese tradition, Buddhaghosa was said to have been himself a *deva*. A great Burmese monk traveled to his heavenly realm through the use of meditation and petitioned him to enter the human realm for the purposes of spreading the *Dharma* (teaching or universal law). For the sake of the *Dharma*, he agreed and was born as an Indian Brahmin. In this Burmese tradition, Buddhaghosa is presented as more than merely precocious. He had memorized the Vedas by the age of seven and demonstrated insight beyond all other Brahmins by the end of his childhood. Upon finding his true identity and after converting to Buddhism, he set out for Sri Lanka in order to translate the canon and commentaries. On his boat trip he was asked by a fellow passenger to solve the riddle: *How does one untangle the tangle with which one is entangled?* In order to pass the time he did so, but a *deva* stole this first copy. Immediately he wrote a second copy and, to ensure its safety, he used it as a pillow. This did not stop the *deva* from stealing even this. By lamplight he then wrote a third copy, whereupon the *deva* then returned the other two copies. Again, all three copies agreed letter to letter.

While the legendary quality of these biographies stretches Western credulity, we surely get the point. *The Path of Purification* is regarded by Theravadin Buddhists as inspired and definitive. While Buddhaghosa is typically described as a teacher of unequaled brilliance, erudition, and clarity, in both these legendary traditions it is clear that it is *The Path of Purification* that is regarded as destined. Possibly the fact that there are virtually no studies on the historical Buddhaghosa or even on *The Path of Purification* reflects this. Another reason that there is so little scholarship on this seminal text is that it is less a creative document as it is an arrangement of essentially classical doctrines. From a Theravada Buddhist's perspective, Buddhaghosa is a monk and scholar who preserved and articulated the Buddhist path clearly and succinctly. It is for this reason that I have chosen him an able dialogue partner for Saint John of the Cross, and I have limited his contribution to this singular tome, *The Path of Purification*.

2/ 2061331.

Notes

1. Jacques Dupuis, *Toward a Christian Theology of Religious Pluralism* (Maryknoll, NY: Orbis, 1997) and Roger Haight, *Jesus Symbol of God* (Maryknoll, NY: Orbis, 1999).

2. Xavier Rynne, *Vatican II* (Maryknoll, NY: Orbis, 1968), 68.

3. The most decisive response came from the Congregation of the Doctrine of the Faith's declaration entitled *"Dominus Iesus: On the Unicity and Salvific Universality of Jesus Christ and the Church* on September 5, 2000," *Origins* 30, no. 14 (2000): 210–219.

4. This is not exactly new. Friedrich Schliermacher raised the bar two hundred years ago. But it is consciously new in much of Catholic theology, particularly poignant in the emerging discipline of theology of religions.

5. See John Paul II, "The Meaning of the Assisi Day of Prayer," *Origins* 16, no. 31 (1987): 561–563, at 562. See also a speech John Paul gave to Indian religious leaders in February 1986 entitled "John Paul II in India: Address to Non-Christian Leaders," *Origins* 15, no. 36 (1986): 597–598, at 597.

6. See, for example, Paul Lakeland's *Postmodernity* (Minneapolis: Augsburg Fortress, 1997); Philip Sheldrake's "The Crisis of Post-Modernity," *Christian Century* (Summer, 1996); and Michael Byron's *The Poor When They See It Will Be Glad: An Ecclesiology of Symbol as Integral to a Socially Relevant Post Modern North American Church* (S.T.D. Diss., Ann Arbor, MI: UMI, 2000), 1–32.

7. Haight, 396.

8. Paul Tillich, *Christianity and the Encounter of the World Religions* (New York: Columbia University Press, 1963), 7.

9. As cited by Paul Knitter, "The Pluralist Move and Its Critics," *Drew Gateway* 58, no. 1 (1989): 1.

10. John Paul II, *Crossing the Threshold of Hope* (New York: Knopf, 1994), 84–90.

11. See Hans Urs von Balthasar, "Christian and Non-Christian Meditation," *Word and Spirit* 1 (1979): 147–166. See also "Buddhism: An Approach to Dialogue," *Communio: International Catholic Review* 15, no. 4 (1988): 403–410.

12. Paul Knitter does an excellent job of presenting a concise version of this position. See *No Other Name? A Critical Survey of Christian*

Attitudes toward the World Religions (Maryknoll, NY: Orbis, 1985), 37–54.

13. See, for example, Rudolf Otto, *The Idea of the Holy* (New York: Oxford University Press, 1958); Fredrich Heiler, "The History of Religions as a Preparation for the Co-operation of Religions," in *The History of Religions: Essays in Methodology*, eds. Eliade and Kitagawa, (Chicago: University of Chicago Press: 1959), 132–160; Saruepalli Radhakrishnan, *The Hindu Life* (New York: Macmillan, 1973), 306–339; and Earnest Hocking, "The Way of Thomas," in *Attitudes toward Other Religions*, ed. Thomas (London: SCM Press, 1969), 133–149. I was originally directed to these volumes by Knitter's *No Other Name?*

14. William James, *Varieties of Religious Experience* (New York: American Library of World Literature, 1958), 380–381.

15. See John Hick, *Problems of Religious Pluralism* (London: Macmillan, 1985), 80; John Hick, "Jesus and the World Religions," in *The Myth of God Incarnate*, ed. Hick (London: SCM Press, 1977), 182; Aloysius Pieris, "Christianity and Buddhism in Core-to-Core Dialogue," *Cross Currents* 37, no. 1 (1975): 47–48; Antony Fernando, "Salvation and Liberation in Buddhism and Christianity," *Lumen Vitae* 27, no. 2 (1972): 306–7.

16. See "What Does Comparative Religion Compare? The Buddhist-Christian Example," *Studies in Religion/Sciences religieuses* 19, no. 2 (1990): 163–171, at 165.

17. Colin Thompson, *The Poet and Mystic: A Study of the Cantico Espiritual of San Juan de la Cruz* (New York: Oxford University Press, 1977), 161.

18. I have found some texts that claim to derive their teaching only from the Pali canon, but on even a superficial reading one finds in them Buddhaghosa's outline from his *Path of Purification*.

19. V. P. Vineeth, "Dialogue and Theology of Religious Pluralism: Theological Reflections," *Journal of Dharma* 14, no. 4 (1989): 282–283. See also Paul Tillich, "Christianity Judging itself in the Light of Its Encounter with the World Religions," in *Christianity and Other Religions: Selected Readings*, eds. Hick and Hebblewaite (Philadelphia: Fortress Press, 1980), 121.

20. Vineeth, 386–387.

21. Harry Hoeler, "Dialogue: Towards a Definition," *The Unitarian Universalist Christian* 45, no. 2–4 (1990): 117. See also Bhikku Parekh,

"The Concept of Inter-Faith Dialogue," *Faith and Freedom* 42, no. 1 (1989): 5.

22. John Cobb, *Beyond Dialogue: Toward a Mutual Transformation of Christianity and Buddhism* (Philadelphia: Fortress Press, 1982), xi.

23. Thomas Merton, *The Asian Journal* (New York: New Directions, 1973), 313.

24. Paul Ingram, "Two Western Models of Interreligious Dialogue," *Journal of Ecumenical Studies* 26, no. 1 (1989): 27; Stanley Samartha, "The Progress and Promise of Interreligious Dialogues," *Journal of Ecumenical Studies* 9, no. 3 (1972): 473–474; Paul Knitter, "Horizons on Christianity's New Dialogue with Buddhism," *Horizons* 8, no. 1 (1981): 41–42; Raimundo Panikkar, "The Myth of Pluralism: The Tower of Babel—a Dedication on Non-violence," *Cross Currents* 29, no. 2 (1979): 200, and Michael Amaladoss, "The Spirituality of Dialogue," *Studies in Interreligious Dialogue* 3, no. 1 (1993): 60.

25. Augustine Morris, "Buddhist-Christian Monastic Contemplative Encounter," *Buddhist-Christian Studies* 9 (1989): 253.

26. Swami Abhishiktananda [Father Henri Le Saux], "The Experience of God in Eastern Religions," *Cistercian Studies* 9, nos. 2–3 (1974): 149. Abhishiktananda has argued that Hinduism is not really a set of ideas but a religion of experience. See also Robert Florida, "What Does Comparative Religion Compare: The Buddhist-Christian Example," *Studies in Religion/Sciences religieuses* 19, no. 2 (1990): 167–171.

27. Donald Mitchell, "A Revealing Dialogue," *The Way Supplement* 78 (Fall 1993): 47–49.

28. See John Berthrong, "Trends in Contemporary Buddhist-Christian Dialogue," *Ecumenical Trends* 14, no. 9 (1985): 136; Joseph Burgess, "Purpose, Problems, and Possibilities of Interreligious Dialogue," *Drew Gateway* 58, no. 3 (1989): 18, and Julius Lipner, "The 'Inter' of Interfaith Spirituality," *The Way Supplement*, 78 (Fall 1993): 66–68.

29. The most important initial modern study of Saint John of the Cross was done by Bruno de Jesus-Marie. See *Saint Jean de la Croix*, revised and corrected from the 1929 edition (Paris: Plon, 1948). This was followed up by the most critical study to date by Crisógono de Jesús Sacramento, *San Juan de la Cruz, vida y obras* (Madrid: Biblioteca de Autores Cristianos, 1955). I am relying on this text in its translated form

by Kathleen Pond (London: Longmans, 1958). The following biographical material is taken from these.

30. Thomas Kane, *Gentleness in John of the Cross* (Oxford: SLG Press, 1985), 1. See also Olivier Leroy, *"Quelques traits de Saint Jean de la Croix comme maitre spirituelle,"* Carmelus 11 (1964), 7–8.

31. Crisógono, 309–310. See also Frederico Ruiz, et al., *God Speaks in the Night: The Life, Times and Teachings of St. John of the Cross* (Washington, DC: ICS Publications, 1991), vi–vii.

32. For example, John refers to the *world* as the enemy of the soul and ugly compared to God (*The Ascent of Mount Carmel* I.4.4). Instead of loving others, we seem to be told to withdraw our affection from everything and everyone so as to focus solely on God (*Ascent* II.6.4). And the body is describe as a prison from which we must detach ourselves (*Ascent* I.3.3; I.15.1; II.8.4). Much of this is hyperbole, but even if not, all this seemingly negative language really needs to be put into perspective of his overall agenda.

33. The dating of these texts is highly controversial and somewhat speculative.

34. See, for example, Francis Clooney's analysis of the movement from focusing on the action of the sacrifice to that of the transcendent reality of the *atman* (transcendent self) as performer of the sacrifice in *Thinking Ritually: Rediscovering the Purva Mimanmsa of Jaimini* (Vienna: Gerold & Co., 1990), 221ff.

35. Given the fact that there is no consistent Hindu theology and that there was a vast array of Hindu practices and texts, it is debated just how unique the Buddha's challenge was to Hindu anthropology. One could also say that the Buddha did not diverge from all Hindu beliefs regarding the nature of liberation, but that he brought an emphasis that took liberation in a different direction. Principally, however, I believe that it is generally accurate to suggest that he challenged fundamentally broad Hindu understandings in both.

36. The Buddha did not speak Sanskrit, the textual language of Mahayana Buddhism, or Pali, the textual language of the Theravada tradition. In what I hope is a less confusing presentation to the Western reader, I use the most common terms with which Westerners are familiar in the Sanskrit language, including *karma* (Pali: *kamma*), *Nirvana* (Pali: *Nibbana*), and *dharma* (Pali: *dhamma*). Less familiar technical terms are generally rendered in the Pali that Buddhaghosa properly used.

37. I am principally relying on Bimala Charan Law's *The Life and Work of Buddhaghosa* (Delhi: Nag Publishers, 1976) and on E. W. Adikaram's *The Early History of Buddhism in Ceylon* (Dehiwala, Sri Lanka: Buddhist Cultural Centre, 1946).

Chapter Two

On Being Human: Anthropologies East and West

Who Are We?

There is an Islamic story about the famous mystic and holy fool Nasruden, who was riding on a donkey through the town square. But his hands were not on the reins, so he went wherever the donkey was interested in going, these interests changing moment to moment. That is, he was wandering aimlessly on a donkey who was aimless. Someone called out, "Nasruden, where are you going?" And he replied, "How should I know, you'll have to ask my donkey." As was typical of this medieval prophet, his often comic actions were a critique on the way most people lived, aimlessly wandering through life. Buddhists call this wandering unenlightened state of existence *samsara*. We wander during life, and we wander from lifetime to lifetime.

In a less clever but just as penetrating way, we have in the West a dictum from Socrates: "The unexamined life is not worth living." This is particularly true for our spiritual lives. Who are we? Where did we come from, and where are we going? What are we made for? Do we have souls, and what are they? What is the relationship between body and soul? What is our relationship to the world? To ourselves? To God? What is the fundamental human problem that a spiritual life tries to address? What is the fundamental human hope that a spiritual life promises to fulfill?

Along with most religions, Christianity and Buddhism attend to these questions in various ways, both philosophically and theologically. The answers they provide fundamentally dictate how we perceive what it means to be saved, liberated, holy, enlightened, and so on. The purpose of this chapter is to analyze what it means to be human from a theological point of view. This is known as *theological anthropology*, and we shall see that Christians and Buddhists have very different anthropologies. Much of what we see in the following pages is technical, but it behooves us to wade through it in order to get a clear understanding of how we ought to go about engaging the spiritual path (chapter 3) and fulfilling our destiny (chapter 4).

The Anthropology of Saint John of the Cross

Sensory and Spiritual Faculties

Saint John understands the human being as having two essential parts, the sensory and the spiritual. But this (scholastic) division in no way suggests that he's dualistic in his understanding of our nature. It is the whole human being that he regularly refers to as a *soul*, and the soul is an integrated reality. He calls it a *suppositum*, a unified whole or one essential being, each part being interrelated to the other.[1] The sensory part possesses what we normally call the five senses. He also includes the soul's use of the imagination as part of the sensory faculties.[2] The sensory part of the soul acts as the window to the world.[3] It is the senses that encounter the world moment to moment, either as satisfying and pleasurable or as unsatisfying and painful. This information is then translated to the spiritual part of the soul, that is, the intellect, the memory, and the will. The spiritual part of the soul is what we would normally call the *psyche*.

The intellect works as we might imagine it to. Principally, it knows by the experience of the senses. The senses give us information about the nature of the world and our participation in it.

This information is processed variously. The intellect takes the information so as to ascertain how to act in the world rationally. The memory stores our experience for future reference. And the will determines what to desire to seek in our experience. Like many of his contemporaries, Saint John's understanding of the process of knowing follows the thought of Saint Thomas.[4]

Really, all three elements of the psyche work together. The memory recalls that which has been stored in the interior part of the soul. It has the ability to recall the past and to retrieve what one has already learned or experienced. It retains all images used by the intellect. This could include graces given by God (even supernatural communications) when they are given to the soul in an intelligible way.[5] The intellect brings information from the memory to understanding and provides rationality for life. The intellect is our guide.[6] The relationship between intellect and memory is critical for John. The memory recalls for the mind images or past experiences, judgments, and predispositions or intellectual habits. Thus, memory has a reciprocal affect with the intellect's operations. It constitutes a paradigm or framework of reference for the intellect to understand. Simply stated, what we remember affects how we understand, judge, and respond to experience.[7]

The will assesses how the soul relates to the information of the senses. Our will naturally inclines toward something we perceive as good. In this sense, our will works like that of other animals and is itself morally neutral.[8] The will is central to one's moral operation. John writes, "When the will directs these faculties, passions, and appetites toward God, turning away from what is not God, the soul preserves its strength for God and comes to love him with all its might."[9] As will become clear, the will is the final arbiter and governor of the whole personality.

In his understanding of the will, John of the Cross utilizes a philosophical principle that is crucial to his logic of spiritual purification: Nature cannot tolerate a void.[10] So when anything is removed, another fills up that space. The issue is not that the senses become filled and so leave no room for God. Rather, the will becomes full when it is attached to the experiences of the sensory part of the soul. John refers to the soul as having an attachment whenever the will is controlled or inordinately influenced by the information given by the senses.[11] So when our affections are purified of all attachments, then they are free to be singularly devoted to God and filled by God, even as we concretely embrace the world.

A second principle following the first is that two contraries cannot coexist at the same time in the same subject.[12] Again, God and the world are not contraries as such. The contraries have to do with our attachments. In this sense, in terms of what the will can be attached to or driven toward, God and the world are on the same plane. And attachment to anything that is not God acts as an impediment to loving God wholeheartedly, and being fully available to God.

In John's anthropology, we have two basic issues to consider. The first is that if we want to be holy, our faculties have to desire and seek union with God, renouncing any attachments to the world, our relationships, and even our idea of ourselves. Being deeply engaged in the world and having loving and primary relationships with others are not problems in the spiritual life. In fact, they are imperatives of the gospel. The problem comes when our soul clings to them or replaces God with them. Second, our faculties, be they sensory or spiritual, are *naturally* geared to the natural world. And God is often mediated through the world, such as nature, our relationships, even scripture and the church. But, of course, God is not a part of this world; he transcends it. So how do the faculties of the human being relate directly to God himself if they are made for negotiating the things of the world? John's answer is through the theological virtues of faith, hope, and love. By grace and through these virtues, the soul's faculties can operate no longer in a *natural* way, but in a *supernatural* way.

Theological Virtues and Spiritual Faculties

Faith and the Intellect

Faith is a tricky term, which we use in a variety of ways. John too uses it variously. Sometimes he simply utilizes the traditional scholastic understanding of faith as a virtue of assent to revealed propositions of the church.[13] Faith can also describe openness and surrender to God in Christ.[14]

Primarily the term *faith* is used by John to refer to that which God does to the soul in contemplative prayer. Faith blinds the intellect of any other knowledge. In the contemplative life, God will empty the intellect of what it naturally knows so that God, who transcends our intellect, can reveal himself uniquely to the soul. Faith is not anti-knowing, for it illuminates the intellect. But it is a knowing that is of a different mode to the natural operations of the intellect, and thus normal ways of understanding. John does not dispute the legitimacy of faith articulations like the creed, but he is convinced that they are limited and that they form a kind of obstacle if one clings to them and remains closed to the deeper understanding and mystery of God himself.[15]

It is the theological virtue of faith that brings the soul to this supernatural understanding of God in contemplation, and therefore, it is the means for direct union of the intellect with God. Faith becomes the vehicle bringing the soul to a higher knowledge and wisdom of God.[16] This higher wisdom is known as *infused knowledge*, that is, supernatural wisdom or knowledge that the soul receives passively, beyond the natural workings of the intellect.

Hope and the Memory

In a like manner, the theological virtue of hope empties the memory of how God *seemed* to the soul in the past, or how the soul approached God, or further, how God *ought* to be considered from what the soul could imagine. In what one does to prepare for union with God, what I later describe as an *active night*, John

31

teaches that we must let go of all things of the memory in prayer, and withdraw affection from anything that is not God.[17] This detachment is primarily in contemplative prayer, but not exclusively. To a lesser degree, he advises a regular practice of removing oneself from resting in the memory. We are, in a word, *recollected.* There is a Zen mantra that fits perfectly with John's teaching on being recollected: "Where are you now?" Of course we experience memories, and this is not a problem. But the active withdrawal of memory in hope means being open moment to moment to a deeper experience of God. And it means not letting our memory limit or dictate our future experience of God. Such recollection keeps the mind present, available, and free for God.

In John's logic, detachment from the memory serves somewhat different purposes than did the detachment of the intellect. His understanding of memory is that it relates to the whole of one's past experience. And not only this, it also relates to one's sense of future possibilities. We can only imagine a future based on our past. The memory provides one's orientation as a historical being. It provides one's identity or perceived identity.[18] To be free for the mystery of God (and one's deepest self), the soul must leave behind all props and walk in this darkness of theological hope.

John writes, "Hope always pertains to the unpossessed object."[19] Since the normal, natural operation of the memory is centered on what has in some sense already been possessed, the theological virtue of hope places the soul in a kind of darkness and emptiness so as to be available to the God who is that ultimate possession. Hope, as an *infused grace,* takes the form of withdrawing one's memory from all expectations.

Love and the Will

As mentioned previously, the will is the arbiter of the personality for John.[20] The will is either unfree, being enslaved by attachments, or it is free in the grace of God. This freedom is the freedom of love. Love is the theological virtue that transforms the will to love God utterly, and even become transformed into God's very love. John teaches that the very nature of love is that it produces a kind of equality and likeness in the soul.[21] The virtue of love then transforms us into the image of Christ. This virtue not only transforms the soul, but it also represents the very union of the soul in God. The most prominent active cultivation of detachment is in the will, and it is the virtue of love that most makes the soul available to be transformed by God's love.

The challenging and seemingly negative language in much of his writings, such as detachment or withdrawal, is really the flip side of what is possible because of these, that is, pure love. Love is the central feature in John's mysticism.[22] It is *the* transforming agent, and the very end to which we were created. We were made to love. This infused love as a grace from God empties the soul from attachments and communicates divine love directly and beyond the will's natural capacity to receive and respond to such love.

The Anthropology of Buddhaghosa

The Five Aggregates

We saw that John's sense of the human being is broken down into a kind of twofold system: the sense faculties and the spiritual faculties. These spiritual faculties are likewise divided into three operations: the intellect, the memory, and the will. Buddhist anthropology also understands the human being as an interrelated whole of different parts. These Buddhaghosa calls aggregates (*khandhas:* lit., "bundles"). We are a collection of five interrelated parts, and if any of these aggregates is missing there exists no person. The five aggregates not only constitute what it means to be human, but describe one's interior operations as well.

1. *Materiality:* Buddhaghosa describes the materiality aggregate as that which involves all states that have the characteristics of the world. Materiality is simply matter made up of the elements of the universe (earth,

water, fire, and air). The materiality aggregate also includes our senses. It is this aggregate that has the fundamental experience of the created world.[23] It is the initial and primary door to experience.[24]

2. *Feeling:* If the materiality aggregate is made up of matter and senses, the feeling aggregate is the direct receiver of those sense impressions. This determines whether what is being experienced is pleasant, unpleasant, or essentially neutral.

3. *Perception:* The purpose of the perceptions aggregate lies in discriminating more subtle, interior, or mental feelings such as memory or ideas. Like the feeling aggregate, perception attends to the data of the mind as pleasant, unpleasant, or neutral. There is no such thing as a consciousness without perceptions. When the feeling or perception aggregate experiences an attending experience as pleasant, the unenlightened response to this is *desire.* When it is experienced as unpleasant, the response is *aversion.* And when something is experienced as neutral, Buddhaghosa says that this tends to put the mind to sleep.[25]

4. *Mental Formations:* This aggregate involves all volitional activity as well as our emotional aptitudes or psychic dispositions. Our mental formations originate from past *karma.* That is, the effect of our past experiences continues to dispose the person in the present. All mental activity comes from the mental formations aggregate. It is the place of our will and our attention. Buddhaghosa describes the quality of mental formations as profitable, unprofitable, or indeterminate, depending upon whether they are associated with mental states that lead either to or away from what is spiritually wholesome.

5. *Consciousness:* The final aggregate that contributes to the makeup of the human being is that awareness which

puts all of our experiences together. The consciousness aggregate is the most important and complex of the five.[26] Within our consciousness there are entrenched three mental dynamics of all unenlightened minds: greed, hatred, and delusion.[27] It is the mental formations aggregate that acts on these dynamics, even though they are lodged in the consciousness. We shall see below that it is the consciousness aggregate that provides the continuum between rebirths. Buddhaghosa refers to the relationship of the consciousness to the other aggregates as *rebirth-linking*.[28] Consciousness is not only the agent of rebirth, it also provides continuity during one's life.

According to Buddhist anthropology, there is nothing more to the human being than these five interacting, impersonal aggregates. Buddhists argue that humans live under the delusion that there exists a stable, essential self underneath experience. This is brought on by failure to clearly analyze the aggregates. Buddhaghosa describes it this way:

> The materiality aggregate, which is gross being the objective field, [experiences]…matter as desirable and undesirable. Then perception which apprehends the aspects of feeling's objective field since what one feels, one perceives; then formations, which form volitionally [desire] through the means of perceptions; and last consciousness, which these things begin with feeling have as their support, and which dominates them.…Clinging causes them. It is through clinging to matter, through insisting upon interpreting matter, that such a view arises: "This is mine, this is I, this is my self."[29]

Dependent-Origination

Dependent-origination is a critical Buddhist term that refers to the interconnectedness of the aggregates and the way in which all causes affect consciousness, *karma*, and rebirth. By understanding how the consciousness works in dependent-origination, one may come to understand how to break its cycle and be released from the endless wandering of the person from one birth to the next.

Buddhaghosa follows traditional Buddhism's description by attributing ignorance as the primal condition:

> Ignorance conditions volitional [desire] formations,
> Which conditions consciousness,
> Which conditions mental-materiality,
> Which conditions the sixfold base [of physicality],
> Which conditions contact with the world,
> Which conditions feeling,
> Which conditions craving,
> Which conditions clinging,
> Which conditions becoming,
> Which conditions birth,
> Which conditions aging and death,
> Which conditions sorrow and grief.[30]

This is the process of *samsara*, of wandering from one birth to another. We die ignorant of the fundamental truths of impermanence *(anicca)*, no self *(anatta)*, and dissatisfaction *(dukkha)*, and this process produces the desire to be reborn. *Karma* is a product of desire. It is the mental energy that drives consciousness to the next rebirth. One can imagine dependent-origination as the relationship between spokes of a wheel that spin simultaneously, the wheel depending upon all the spokes. While each condition is dependent upon, and in that sense, caused by the previous conditions, no one condition exists without the others. The whole wheel arises and spins together. If one were to take out any condition, the whole wheel would collapse.

To continue the metaphor, ignorance is placed first because it is the only spoke capable of being taken out of the wheel. In the Four Noble Truths, which we saw in chapter 1, the cause of *dukkha* is desire or thirst. This is the central problem of life, and it is based on ignorance of who we ultimately are.[31] Ignorance gives the mental formations no choice but to crave, since they misunderstand the very dynamics of craving. An unenlightened mind naturally craves. And ignorance, he asserts, is the cause of all formations, craving included.[32] One could argue that some people have little love or craving for life. One might even be suicidal. Where's the clinging or desire in this? But aversion to life's experience is itself simply the flip side of desire. We are still identifying with the experience of life, only this time it is identifying with our pain. It is still an attachment.

Karma

I have mentioned *karma* several times but, seeing that it is so central to how Buddhists understand themselves and the world, perhaps a fuller description is in order. We have observed that ignorance is the fundamental issue for rebirth, and that consciousness provides the rebirth-linking aggregate between lives. Further, it is *karma* that produces the energy for the consciousness aggregate to continue lifetime to lifetime. "Good *karma*" leads to a pleasant rebirth, while "bad *karma*" leads to a very unpleasant one.[33] Only when *karma* is halted, however, does one get off the wheel of *samsara*.

In his anthropology, Buddhaghosa attributes a great deal to the dynamics of *karmic* energy. *Karma* both produces the condition that causes rebirth as well as the support for sustaining the human being.[34] The foundational cause of *karma* is ignorance, and in ignorance we experience craving, clinging, and volition.[35] So *karma* is the energy for rebirth and aggregate formation, and it is perpetuated constantly throughout life by the very dynamics of volition it creates. All of this ties together in the mind. When one is ignorant of the three characteristics of all reality, particularly regarding one's selflessness, then one craves. And ironically, the process of craving keeps the mind from seeing clearly these central characteristics.

Such ignorance causes and shapes a craving mind, and thus, even more volitions. This is what Buddhaghosa means by *volition:* an intention involving craving. Someone who is enlightened surely *intends* things. But this intention is neither caused by nor cultivates an attachment or narcissistic clinging. In this sense, it is as though wisdom itself acts. There is no self behind the action, and when one realizes this truth *karma* ceases to be produced. Without *karma* there is no energy in the consciousness aggregate for rebirth-linking. The cessation of creating *karma* is how one escapes the wheel of rebirth and enters *Nirvana.*

Summary

We saw in the first chapter that, according to Theravada Buddhism, all phenomenal reality has the three fundamental characteristics of impermanence *(anicca)*, no self *(anatta)*, and dissatisfaction *(dukkha)*. In terms of Buddhaghosa's presentation, we also now see that this analysis is crucial toward understanding the dynamics of the human being. All the aggregates are impermanent and thus represent interrelated processes that are constantly changing. And they are always being formed by *karma* derived from craving. This is going on all through life. Even in terms of rebirth, there is simply a new formation of the aggregates due to *karmic* energy. Rebirth is a reconstitution of the formations and consciousness aggregates, but even these have the imprint of the others, and thus, all five aggregates cooperate in forming a new rebirth.

In this sense, while rebirth happens only through the last two aggregates, there is no such thing as any aggregate being missing. Their arisings are interdependent. This is the central tenet of dependent-origination. One is tempted to think of the consciousness aggregate as being the *self*, as the being that moves from lifetime to lifetime. Such an interpretation is not Buddhist. It would rather be more amenable to the Hindu notion of reincarnation, or more technically the transmigration of the soul *(atman)*. For the

Buddhist, unlike the Hindu, there simply is no permanent self to reincarnate.

We see three fundamental truths about Buddhist anthropology. These truths, not coincidentally, correspond to the three characteristics of all phenomenal reality. By impermanence *(anicca)*, we see that everything is always in flux. Impermanence teaches that even rebirth is simply another, albeit dramatic, flux of the aggregates. Since they are always in flux, always involved in the dynamics of *anicca*, rebirth is really no different from the moment-to-moment changes that happen even in a given lifetime.

The second truth in dependent-origination concerns no-self *(anatta)*. There is simply no singular, underlying essence of a person. There is only a collection of interrelated, always changing, ever impersonal aggregates, wandering moment to moment, lifetime to lifetime. A crucial element in the Buddhist path to enlightenment involves insight into this doctrine of no-self, so that what appears to be a solid mass is experienced in Buddhist practice as not solid at all. We are simply a collection of impersonal aggregates.

The third truth in dependent-origination is the concept of dissatisfaction *(dukkha)*. This selfless process of life is experienced as *dukkha* when experienced in a manner based on ignorance. Such ignorance gives rise to unwholesome mental formations that need to be eliminated in following the path.

While the Theravada framework of enlightenment hinges on the insight of no-self *(anatta)*, this view that there simply is nothing more to the human being that this impersonal collection, it would be erroneous to conclude that enlightenment means extinction after death. One would also be in error to conclude that there must be a *super-self* or soul not associated with these impersonal changes, as if there was sort of some nonobjectifiable soul. To the Western mindset, it must be one or the other. Either we have a soul, or we do not have a soul. For the Buddhist, this remains an inappropriate question.[36]

To speculate on religious views that are not inherently conducive to the path of enlightenment is considered virtually immoral, since speculations lead away from enlightenment, and not toward it.[37] In this sense, the *dharma* is always considered a path or raft and nothing more. The *dharma* is truth, and Buddhist doctrine holds it without question. But it is a truth about phenomenal existence. It is appropriate only for understanding the phenomenal world. From the point of view of *Nirvana* (a *supramundane* reality), such views no longer apply. There is another problem with the natural tendency to speculate about *Nirvana*, which is that such a speculation leads to a dualistic mindset. The Buddha taught: "This world leans on duality: upon the belief in existence or non-existence....Avoiding these two extremes, the Perfect One shows the doctrine of the middle: Dependent on ignorance are the *karma*-formations....By the cessation of ignorance, *karma*-formations cease."[38]

Anthropologies Compared

Convergences

Constantly Craving

There are striking similarities in the way both John of the Cross and Buddhaghosa view the human condition and the way the will operates. John simply describes the nature of the will before it is reformed in grace as being driven by inordinate appetites. This is not inherent to the structure of the human being, but rather, the disorder of the will due to the original sin. In this sense, the disordered will is normal but not natural. Buddhaghosa's presentation of the disordered will is described in a somewhat more philosophically complex way. Volitions, he teaches, arise from *karma* formations. These formations are produced by the grasping mind and provide the energy for further grasping. Until the delusion is broken by meditative insight, the mind will be forever grasping.

Despite incredible differences in how they believe the human being is constructed, we see that experientially the will operates in essentially the same way. Information is brought from the senses to one's consciousness and experienced as either pleasing or displeasing. An unreformed mind inclines toward or away from experience based on the pleasure principle. Buddhaghosa teaches that all things are conditioned. In terms of the will, the mind is conditioned to incline to or avert from what is experienced. John would agree. We are not aware of the power of our attachments. The mind instantly and spontaneously clings to what it perceives as delightful and runs from whatever is painful.

The quality of clinging to the delightful and averting from the painful can also be appreciated in relation to spiritual experiences. We can be greedy for spiritual experiences that are pleasing and run from those more painful or challenging. Buddhaghosa also teaches that one can become attached to the spiritual bliss found in some meditations, but run away from those practices or experiences that feel afflicting. In both cases, these attachments continue to imprison the person and arrest further spiritual progress.

Delude Ego

Narcissism is a central anthropological issue for both John and Buddhaghosa. Both describe how unwittingly the self makes one the center of all things. For John, God is the true center, and for Buddhaghosa, there is no center. Neither position, however, has any importance for the unreformed will. An unpurified person acts as if he or she were what is truly important or central in the universe. All other beings are only as if satellites revolving around one's life and experience. Christians might say that they love God above all things, or that "Jesus is Lord." But for the unreformed soul, what this usually means is that God has an essential importance for the soul. Until purified, the soul's self-concern remains central.

Nature of Attachments

While we tend to think of our attachments as gratifying or comforting to the soul, are they really? While we may realize that attachments to food or tobacco may not be, in the end, good for us, nonetheless we do have a sense that at least they give us some sense of comfort. But do they? Think about tobacco addiction. One is so often wondering when and where one can have a smoke. One tends to ignore or downplay others' health concerns (They're fanatics). In fact, truth be told, one spends a great deal of mental and physical energy thinking about smoking. What the deluded consciousness believes to be true (Smoking gives me comfort), a more clear perception betrays (Smoking agitates my mind and soul). John finds this dynamic operating with all inordinate appetites. They weary and agitate the soul. They make the soul perpetually seeking and perpetually dissatisfied. Further, since our appetites can never be sated by natural means, the soul is forever seeking more gratification. They can also blind the soul to what is true and truly valuable. What becomes of supreme value in our attached state is simply what feels good to us.[39]

Buddhaghosa's description of the nature and dynamics of inordinate attachments is less detailed in any one place, but it permeates the whole agenda of *The Path of Purification*. The problem that attachments cause is most clearly understood in his description of the dependent-origination. As we saw previously, ignorance is the condition of possibility for the formation of the aggregates. These aggregates in turn condition craving, clinging, and so on.[40] Recall that Buddhaghosa's whole liberative agenda involves cutting off *karma*. *Karma* arises from volitions, that is, intentions that are entrenched in narcissistic attachment.[41] As Buddhaghosa describes it, craving brings sense-desire clinging. This produces, he says, a *fever* for sense-desires and an infatuation with them.[42] But, as we saw, attachments do not stop with sensual desires. Rather the aggregates themselves are objects of clinging.[43] Minimizing and eventually eradicating these attachments, on the other hand, frees the mind of greed and covetousness.[44] In the first chapter of *The Path of Purification,* Buddhaghosa describes virtue as disciplining our attachments and our predilection for clinging. This, he teaches, helps to produce dispassion and the fading of greed. Such a fading brings greater freedom for the mind and allows for the possibility of deliverance.[45]

Remedy as Detachment

In analyzing the problem of the will and the remedies that both John and Buddhaghosa describe, we could also say that they have similar agendas for the will. Buddhaghosa describes the will as needing to be unattached for the purpose of deliverance. Detachment is the condition for the arising of *Nirvana.* John shares that agenda in a theistic way. Recall that nature cannot tolerate a void. Attachments fill this void, which is ultimately meant to be filled only by God. God is not a competitor with the world as such. But in terms of attachments, the will does experience competing interests. For both authors, the emptying of the will of all attachments frees one to be wholly available to the goal of the spiritual quest.

As both agree that interior attachments need to be emptied by the will, they also describe similar preliminary work for this project. That is, the morality of restraint from such things that would disturb one's mind and heart, and thus one's progress. We look at this work in the next chapter. In their spiritual and moral analysis, both John of the Cross and Buddhaghosa view the human predicament essentially identically. The human will strives for that which imprisons it in gratification. And that very imprisoning behavior strengthens the bars of the prison. As we will see in the next chapter, the remedy that they both recommend involves sabotaging those gratifications through renunciation and asceticism. While John describes this process as more painful than does Buddhaghosa, both see the same result. The aspirant is freer, more clear-headed, and more available for spiritual growth.

Divergences

Philosophically, the anthropologies of John of the Cross and Buddhaghosa are utterly different. John understands the human being as a complete whole. In his Thomistic psychology, the soul has different faculties that operate by their own properties and in their own ways. Among them, the spiritual faculties also have the capacity to operate by grace in a supernatural way. But all these various faculties, taken collectively, designate a substantial, personal human being—a soul. This soul is called to love and be united to God completely.

Buddhaghosa, on the other hand, describes the nature of the person as utterly impersonal. There is no super-soul underneath the impermanent, impersonal collection of aggregates. Coming to insight of these truths (*anicca* and *anatta*) is the way the mind breaks from delusion—there is simply no essential self. This is critical not only to Buddhist anthropology but also to the Buddhist project of liberation. One progresses on the path by actively looking for impermanence, no-selfhood, and dissatisfaction in everything, and by interpreting all experience through those characteristics.

The philosophical differences between these two spiritual systems should not be marginalized or readily dismissed, and sometimes they have been. How we understand our very nature affects how we proceed in the spiritual life and how we interpret our experience. One's anthropology plays a major role in our understanding of the very goal of the spiritual life, and this cannot be emphasized enough. There is an enormous difference between believing oneself as made for love and believing oneself to be no-self at all.

Notes

1. See *Dark Night of the Soul* I.4.2. Saint John of the Cross also calls all the faculties of the soul, both the *sensual* and the *spiritual*, a whole harmonious composite—all of which can be employed in love (*Dark Night* II.11.4; *The Spiritual Canticle* 16.5; 16.10; *The Living Flame of Love* 3.7).

2. *The Ascent of Mount Carmel* II.12.1–3.

3. *Ascent* I.3.3.

4. See James Denis Edwards, *The Dynamism in Faith: The Interaction between Experience of God and Explicit Faith: A Comparative Study of the Mystical Theology of St. John of the Cross and the Transcendental Theology of Karl Rahner* (Ph.D. Diss., Ann Arbor, MI: UMI, 1979), 50ff, and Elizabeth Wilhelmsen, *Cognition and Communication in John of the Cross* (New York: Lang, 1985), 6ff.

5. *Ascent* III.2.4; 7.1–2; III.14.1.

6. *Ascent* III.1.1.

7. Wilhelmsen, 31.

8. *Ascent* III.16.2ff.

9. *Ascent* III.16.2.

10. *Ascent* I.4.2; I.6.1–2; II.15.4; *Dark Night* II.5.4; II.9.2.

11. *Ascent* I.6–12.

12. *Ascent* I.4.2; 6.1–2; *Dark Night* II.5.4; 9.2.

13. *Ascent* II.3.1; II.27.1–4.

14. *Ascent* II.1.3; II.3.1–4; III.31.8; *Dark Night* I.11.4; II.2.5.

15. *Ascent* II.3.4; *Dark Night* II.17.2.

16. *Ascent* II.8.6.

17. *Ascent* III.2.4–13.

18. Wilhelmsen, 16.

19. *Ascent* II.6.3.

20. The strength of the soul, he says, is ruled by the will (*Ascent* III.16.2). For an excellent treatment of the will and the role of love, see Edwards, 91–92.

21. *Ascent* I.5.1.

22. *Dark Night* II.5.1; II.11.2; II.12.1–2; II.20.6.

23. Buddhaghosa divides materiality into internal and external, gross and subtle, and inferior and superior levels.

24. *The Path of Purification*, 15.3.

25. I will not spend much time on the experience of that which is neutral, since it is given little attention by Buddhaghosa.

26. Buddhaghosa lists eighty-nine different types of consciousness.

27. *Path*, 14.89.

28. "And after death there is rebirth-linking again; and after rebirth-linking, life continuum. Thus the conscious continuity of beings who hasten through the kinds of becoming, destiny, station, and abode occurs without break" (14.124). See also 17.136.

29. *Path*, 14.213.

30. *Path*, 17.2.

31. *Path*, 17.40–51.

32. *Path*, 17.108–110.

33. Actually, there are various kinds of *karma*, each of which affect the person differently. That is, they *ripen* differently. But this is the general dynamic.

34. *Path*, 11.111. So even enlightened Buddhists have *karmic* energy from their pasts, which support them through life. What distinguishes them from others is that they no longer produce *karma*, and thus, have to endure no more rebirths. See also 17.199; 7.16; 7.19; 17.89. This is true except for the consciousness aggregate. Being the rebirth-linking aggregate, *karma* gives it its energy for rebirth, but the consciousness aggregate is its condition of existence. In this sense, consciousness causes *karma*. Of course, many conscious states are themselves caused by *karma* (17.120ff).

35. *Path*, 17.293.

36. For an overview of different interpretations of the self and the various schools of thought, see Y. Krishan, "Buddhism and Belief in *Atma*," *Journal of the International Association of Buddhist Studies* 7, no. 2 (1984): 117–135. For an overview on some modern Buddhalogists' opinions regarding the self, see Lynn De Silva, *The Problem of Self in Buddhism and Christianity* (Columbo: Study for the Center of Religion and Society, 1975), 50–71.

37. Buddhists have called such speculations *ditthi*, which translates, "views." Of course, there are doctrines in Buddhism that are taken seriously, and on the path they are taken absolutely. But *ditthi* is a pejorative term reflecting an error in procedure. When one is engaged in *ditthi*, one is not engaged skillfully on the path. There is also sometimes

used in the *suttas* a play on words, which reinforces the Buddhist critique of speculations. *Mana* (conceit) is connected to and played off of *mannati* (to conceptualize). See Takeuchi Yoshinori, *The Heart of Buddhism: In Search of the Timeless Spirit of Primitive Buddhism*, ed., trans. Heisig (New York: Crossroad, 1983), 3–7.

38. *Samyutta-Nikaya* 12.15. When charged with being a nihilist, the Buddha responds that he is merely teaching suffering and the cessation of suffering (see the *Alagaddupama Sutta*). Ultimately, the teaching on *anatta* is not about ontology, but liberation.

39. For a complete description, see *Ascent* I.16–12.

40. *Path*, 17.2.

41. The project of getting off of the wheel of *samsara* or rebirth centers on cutting off *karma*. But without renouncing clinging, the wheel continues to spin. Buddhaghosa says that rebirth is caused by ignorance, which leads to craving, to clinging, and necessarily to more *karma* (19.4; 7.15ff).

42. *Path*, 12.242ff.

43. *Path*, 14.214; 14.225.

44. *Path*, 4.87.

45. *Path*, 1.32.

Chapter Three

The Path to Holiness

Where Are We Going?

Several years ago one of my students asked me at lunch if a given ascetical practice was a good idea for Lent. I responded, "It depends how holy you want to be." Someone else at the table, a woman trained in spiritual direction, countered, "No, it depends on where the Holy Spirit is leading you." In many ways her response was better than mine. My response appeared to border on works righteousness—as if we can make ourselves holy—while her response focused on letting God and his grace lead the way. One could also argue that my response sounded a bit elitist, while hers was one of being humbly solicitous to the movements of the Holy Spirit in the soul. Actually, the difference in our approaches had more to do with our backgrounds. Hers was decidedly Ignatian, that is, based on the spiritual principles of Ignatius of Loyola. This is a spirituality that vigorously resists any attempt to present spirituality or holiness in a clear-cut "one size fits all" mentality. Rather, we let God teach us how we are to become holy, each person being uniquely led by the Spirit. I personally believe that this is a spirituality most people resonate with.

In contrast to this more open-ended spirituality, there are some spiritual paths that are more linear. This is where I was coming from in my response. In contemplative spiritualities like Saint John's, there is a progression that one can mark. One can even predict, in general terms, future experiences. Saint Teresa of Avila's spirituality, also Carmelite, is also essentially linear. In her greatest book, *The Interior Castle*, Teresa describes seven stages of interior prayer and purification. It's not that holiness is automatic or something we can control, for only grace can make one holy, or even progress for that matter. Rather, it is that some paths have a predictable progress and make quite specific demands.

Seven years ago I was speaking to a student who had many of the signs of early contemplation in her life. These I knew from the writings of Saint John of the Cross, Saint Teresa of Avila, and *The Cloud of Unknowing*. I told her that she was entering this path, and her response was, "I don't even like that kind of spirituality. It's too individualistic and dualistic for me." She was married and decidedly committed to a conjugal spirituality she could share with her husband. "Too bad," I half-jokingly replied, "you're on it." And I could essentially predict her spiritual progress over the next several years. Since that fateful conversation, we have, in fact, found her spiritual progress to be virtually textbook according to the Carmelite tradition. It is almost as if John's writings were her very own journal.

Both John and Buddhaghosa describe this kind of spiritual dynamic, one that is progressive and essentially linear. In fact, I believe that Buddhaghosa would think his presentation of the path to be typical for every Buddhist. John would not be so presumptuous, but he does have a great deal of confidence that for those who are called to a contemplative spirituality, there is a standard path of progression.[1]

Saint John's Path to Union with God

The Nights of the Senses

The Active Night of the Senses

In the Prologue of *The Ascent of Mount Carmel*, John describes why he wrote the book and for whom it is intended. His purpose was to alert souls to what may be happening to them as God brings them into the contemplative life. John says that he wants to keep souls from spiritually regressing, and to help them learn to embrace the kinds of abandonment and nights into which God is inviting them.[2] He states that his doctrine will not be accessible to everyone, but to those "whom God favors by putting on the path leading to this mount [of union]....Because they are already detached to a great extent from the temporal things of the world, they will more easily grasp this doctrine on nakedness of spirit."[3]

Even though John wrote about what he believed to be essentially a universal way toward a universal supernatural goal—union with God—he believed that it is not entirely accessible or even understandable to all.[4] One has to be somewhat on the road for it to make sense. His starting point is with people who are already substantially practicing a rigorous spiritual life of detachment from gratifications and who are living a life of prayer. John calls these souls *beginners.*

Beginners are not beginners in the spiritual life in general. They are religious and lay people who have been serious about their spiritual lives and are deeply committed. Beginners know and love God truly. But John is critical of beginners. While they are authentically spiritual at some level, he believed that the focus of their spiritual lives is unconsciously the gratification of the self. As we saw in the previous chapter, personal satisfaction is the essential motivating force behind a beginner's piety.[5] There is a kind of spiritual narcissism that dominates the beginner's life.[6]

A beginner truly experiences God's grace and truly knows God. But such a knowledge and relationship is based on a *sensible* life. Recall from chapter 2 that the standard operations of the soul takes the mode of negotiating in the natural world. God is present in our world, but our experience of God is mediated through this mode. John describes their spiritual experience as that of eating "morsels" from God's table, or of eating the "rind" of the fruit instead of the heart of the fruit itself.[7] In addition, beginners still have many attachments that need to be confronted. At this time, beginners do not realize their inherent spiritual limitations. Some may even think themselves in full possession of the Lord. In John's critique of the spiritual attachments of beginners, spiritual pride is the foremost disorder.[8]

Because the beginner is still a novice in the contemplative life, and because there is still a great attachment to inordinate desire, John recommends that the soul act in three primary ways. First, one should imitate Christ. This involves learning about his life and examples of self-giving, and behaving as one thinks he would. Second, the soul is to mortify the appetites by depriving them of gratifications of anything not purely for the honor and glory of God. The appetites that cause attachments to the soul are of particular importance. Third, the soul needs to mortify natural passions, pride, and disordered desires by striving toward humility. John says that we do this with an honest self-awareness and by cultivating a sense of our own lowliness before God and the world.[9] This is the *active night of the senses*. This night of the senses refers to withdrawing from the very comforts and attachments on which we generally rely. And it is labeled an *active* night in that it refers to what one actively does to dispose oneself to the more powerful graces of God.

The Passive Night of the Senses

According to John, the typical posture of anyone serious about the spiritual life ought to be one of asceticism and humility. In his overall path, it is also a prelude and a cultivated openness to receiving contemplative graces. God had been speaking to the soul in a sensory way. That is, the soul finds God as mediated through such things as nature, life-giving relationships, and the inspiration one feels in meditation or mental prayer. As we have seen, though, this is just a "morsel" of God. When God begins to offer the soul a contemplative knowledge of himself, he speaks to the soul more directly. And this means that he ceases to communicate through the senses or through the imagination as before. As a result, the world of ordinary prayer and meditation becomes dry, since the sensory satisfactions no longer accompany prayer as they previously had.[10] The primary reason for the experience of dryness is that the spiritual faculties are not sensitized to this more interior and subtle encounter that God is now giving the soul.[11]

In two places of his writings, John offers signs to know whether or not this dryness in prayer is due to God's infused grace or to other psychological factors.[12] In both cases he says that it is imperative for all three signs to be present. In *The Ascent of Mount Carmel*, the three signs are (1) one cannot make discursive meditation or receive satisfaction from it as before; (2) one lacks the desire to fix one's imagination on any other thing in the world; and (3) one desires to stay in simple loving awareness of God without particular considerations. This third sign is the most critical. In *Dark Night*, the three signs are (1) one finds no satisfaction or consolation from God or any other creature; (2) one turns to God solicitously and with painful care; and (3) one finds an inability to use the imagination in prayer. I find that these signs are essentially the same with one caveat. In *The Ascent* the soul enjoys remaining in loving awareness of God, while in *Dark Night* the soul is described as being in anguish without any sense of God. But these can be easily reconciled. We must remember that the beginner finds this experience so new and the graces so subtle and delicate by comparison to what was previously known that one may have little to no awareness that contemplative graces are even being communicated. To the degree that this is initially unrealized, this new contemplative prayer feels very dry. Conversely, to the degree that one can intuit this new mode of grace, one finds a kind of enjoyment in simply resting in God's love.

The passive night of the senses is a process whereby God brings sensible dryness to the soul. This is not a continuous experience, and at first hardly noticeable. Souls think that they are only experiencing a poignant solicitude for God.[13] But as one progresses through this passive night, one experiences increasing awareness of God's general loving presence.[14] The passive night of the senses may be painful and dry to the *sensory* part of the soul, but it is also energizing the *spiritual* part.[15] That is, one's interior faith life literally feels as though it is infused with new power and energy. Indeed, it has.

This dark night brings one into the stage of progress whereby one is a *proficient*. Traditionally, this has been described as the "illuminative way." The soul lives many years as a proficient, becoming increasingly liberated. One readily finds within serene, loving contemplation and spiritual delight.[16] Proficients become increasingly attuned to a whole realm of the spiritual life, which their preoccupation with sensory experience had previously blocked. What had been a vague awareness of God continues to intensify even periodically into more powerful experiences of prayerful absorption in God's love.[17]

The passive night of the senses is not something that the soul does positively, but what God does exclusively. It is God who detaches the soul from interest in a sensory approach to prayer. The major effect of the night of the senses is that the proficient, unlike the beginner, is far less motivated in the religious life by a need for personal satisfaction in spiritual practice. One is thereby enabled to act truly selflessly rather than for personal gratification. It is, above all, a matter of motivational change. Thus, the night of the senses leads to deeper prayer and more authentic ministry, since one is no longer compromised by self-interest.

Experience of the Purgation of the Senses

The active and passive nights of the senses are described by John as both bitter and freeing. There are privations that are trying to the soul, but these very privations open one to deeper, richer experiences of both God and oneself. The soul also sees more clearly how deluded one was in one's attachments. While they were previously experienced as giving the soul security, these very attachments are now seen to the soul as the very things that imprison it. One comes now to a much greater self-awareness as well as a great dependence on God. Freed from our pride and addictions to pleasure, we now find a greater love for others.

John provides an insightful critique of how our attachments, which we indulge to provide emotional comfort and security, actually cause restlessness, anxiousness, and insecurity of spirit. The nights of the senses, especially the passive night, is an experience of deep freedom for the soul. Of course, the experience of asceticism is at first challenging. But after this initial shock comes much greater peace.

As a result of the nights of the senses, proficients grow in a deep knowledge and experience of God. What was almost unnoticeable at first, or an experience of painful concern and solicitude for God, increasingly becomes an awareness of the presence of a general loving knowledge of God.[18] This knowledge can even blossom at times into profound experiences of spiritual absorption, which John calls "touches of union."[19]

The Nights of the Spirit

The Active Night of the Spirit

The approach that John takes toward the night of the senses follows his belief that God desires to lead souls to communicate with him more interiorly and more directly. God can be appreciated, loved, and experienced through the senses (including the imagination), but this is, as I have said, similar to eating the rind and not the substance of the fruit. Since the sensory faculties are limited in their natural operations to sensible experiences, they do not have the capacity to encounter God directly. Rather, our knowledge of God in our lives is indirect and mediated. Further, since the beginner is still spiritually narcissistic and attached to sensory experience, there has to be an emptying of the sensory life in prayer. This is the same approach he takes for the spiritual part of the soul. As with the sensory faculties, the spiritual faculties— intellect, memory, and will—are limited in and of themselves in their natural operations. The difference is that the spiritual faculties do have the capacity to know God directly in an infused or supernatural way.

John is clear that all spiritual progress is at God's initiative. The beginner is led into contemplation by God's bidding, and so too is the proficient led into the *night of the spirit*. However, one can prepare for this initiative. Just as the beginner had previously practiced active forms of sensory detachment in order to be ready for the passive night of the sense, so too does the proficient practice an *active night of the spirit* before God draws the soul into the actual passive night of the spirit.

For the many years when souls are proficients, they habitually let go of their conceptual understandings of God. They practice for years a more general loving knowledge of God in their prayer life. In short, we have ideas of who God is and how God works, and these need to be set aside in prayer. The will is active in practicing increased solicitude to God and averting from one's attachments, and the soul continues to strive to desire what God desires. In terms of the memory, which is so important in assisting the imagination in meditation, the soul has been practicing its own kind of emptiness in prayer. One sets aside expectations of how God will speak to or be with the soul. There is a kind of radical openness and emptiness that the will practices so that God, who is absolute mystery, can speak as God would speak more directly as he actually is.

The Passive Night of the Spirit

While the proficient has been practicing a kind of withdrawal in prayer and an emptying recollection in one's day-to-day life, nothing can really prepare for God's grace in what comes next. This passive night of the spirit is what God does to truly empty the soul. John describes it as a purging and an illumination of the entire soul in a radical way.[20] This is the transition period from being a proficient to entering into union. And this should be understood as entirely God's work. God personally empties the spiritual faculties so that the soul feels completely paralyzed in its natural operations. John writes:

It [the passive night of the spirit] puts the sensory and spiritual appetites to sleep, deadens them, and deprives them of the ability to find pleasure in anything. It binds the imagination and impedes it from doing any good discursive work. It makes the memory cease, the intellect becomes dark and unable to understand anything, and hence it causes the will also to become arid and constrained, and all the faculties empty and useless.[21]

The dark night of the spirit is the most intense and difficult period for the soul in the spiritual journey. He considers this process as that which leads to the soul's *espousal* to God. This night is not a singular experience, but often lasts for years.[22] John's advice for this period is for the soul to absolutely abandon itself in faith, hope, and love, to sustain itself through devotion and prayer in God's often perceived absence, and to be comforted in one's suffering with the knowledge that God is both in control and trustworthy. John repeatedly reminds us that this same light, which can be experienced as painful and blinding, is also the light of union.[23]

In this dark night, the soul is engaged in contemplation to a high degree. There is a kind of knowledge given to the soul, but it cannot be grasped by the natural intellect, and one is to do nothing except to receive it passively.[24] While the soul is not working with its natural potentials, this is not to say that the spiritual faculties are dulled during this time. On the contrary, they are very alert, attentive to and receiving deep levels of *dark wisdom* and knowledge from God.[25]

There is a continuity between the nights of the senses and spirit; they do not exist as utterly separate movements on the spiritual path. At the outset of his writings, John alludes to the fact that even in the nights of the sense, there is an experience of the nights of the spirit.[26] Further, it is only during the passive night of the spirit that our purification from attachments, which was the focus of the active night of the sense, really happens. What seemed in the active night of the spirit to be a cutting off of our attachments, we see now was just a pruning. Now they are cut off at the roots.[27] The nights of the senses and spirit can be likened to two interrelated realities that are part of the same process. Of course, it is also logical to see that one's moral life and the need for initial purification is the first to be addressed. In the experience of purification, however, they cannot be really separated.[28]

Experience of the Nights of the Spirit

The active night of the spirit is challenging to the soul in much the same way as the active night of the senses. It requires detachment from that which has heretofore given the soul comfort and security, albeit a false one. This detachment now, however, is from the intellectual supports and comfortable paradigms in which one understood oneself, God, and the world. In the nights of the spirit, the soul becomes disabused of the false identity it has cultivated and of a limited, and sometimes distorted, understanding of God. Last, the illusion through which the soul so narcissistically appropriated the world, as though it revolved around the soul, is betrayed. While this night is also freeing, as was the night of the senses, one also encounters a painful loss of equilibrium. One confronts what Thomas Merton often called the *false self*, that is, the very ego identity we have built up over a lifetime.[29]

The nights of the spirit have no parallel in human experience. In comparing the nights of the spirit to that of the senses, John writes, "This purgation is more obscure, dark, and dreadful."[30] Because God is working in the soul powerfully and directly, the soul feels great suffering. God, who is love, is not the cause of pain exactly; rather it is one's imperfections being purified that make the soul suffer. In the dark night of the spirit, the soul feels itself in an utterly hopeless and paradoxical situation. Christ's love is what the soul desires, but, due to the intensity of the grace experienced and the weakness and limited capacity of the soul, that very love often feels painful to receive. And the irony continues. John says that when these particularly painful experiences of

God's *anointing* pass, the soul feels alone, empty, and weak. In other words, even though the soul wishes to withdraw while under the siege of God's love, as soon as such a siege subsides, the soul longs for the very presence of God whose presence seemed so painful.[31]

Not all experiences of the nights of the spirit are challenging. Even before one comes to the state of union one may have profound, but not overwhelming, experiences of God's love. In fact, one definition of contemplation John employs is *noticia amorosa*—noticing love. It is an encounter and recognition of the divine presence in one's life as love.[32] Sometimes these experiences are incredibly subtle and delicate, delighting the soul throughout; even, he says, to the very points of our fingers.[33] Other times this love is not so subtle. John uses the image of an assailing arrow or dart afire with the love of the Holy Spirit. When the soul is pierced with that dart, the flame of love gushes forth with sudden ascent and the soul feels unsurpassable delight. The soul, he says, feels as though the entire universe is a sea of love in which it is engulfed.[34]

Buddhaghosa's Path to *Nirvana*

It is, above all, the *path* in which all Buddhist doctrine and values are to be understood.[35] While Buddhists believe that their doctrine is an accurate reflection of reality, it is principally understood in a functional way. Doctrine points to *how* one becomes enlightened. Buddhaghosa writes, "When a wise man, established well in virtue, develops consciousness and understanding, then as a monk ardent and sagacious, he succeeds in disentangling the tangle."[36] This is the beginning of *The Path of Purification*. It is the shorthand answer to the riddle: *How does one untangle the tangle with which one is entangled?* Establishing oneself in virtue and developing consciousness and understanding is the way, and indeed the key, to understanding Buddhism. The rest of his *Path of Purification* is his detailed description of this shorthand answer.

Buddhaghosa also writes in his Introduction that the one who disentangles the tangle possesses six things: virtue, concentration, the threefold understanding (impermanence, no-selfhood, and dissatisfaction), and ardor. Thus, with ardor presumed, his aim is to describe how virtue, concentration, and understanding lead to enlightenment.[37] This is the way.

Virtue *(Sila)*

The essential path to enlightenment is a meditative one, as we shall see, but it first depends upon training in virtue. While virtue is universally regarded as the logical foundation of all serious spiritual growth, in Buddhism it is also understood as the essential basis for providing the mental culture for meditation.[38] In his treatment of virtue, Buddhaghosa presumes a monastic audience. This means that in addition to the five moral precepts that all Buddhists observe, there exist 227 rules ordering the lives of his readers.[39] The ethos of the rules is that of providing a mental culture of restraint to the senses.[40]

Some of these rules of virtue include proscriptions against subtle levels of misconduct, while others have to do with ascetical principles, such as wearing used clothing (literally rags), eating from a singular begging bowl, living under a tree, and even refraining from lying down. Their purpose, he says, is to "eliminate sensual desire since they manifest the opposite."[41] Buddhaghosa writes that, while ascetic practices are profitable, they are particularly important for those temperaments that are greedy or deluded. While ascetic practices may be considered challenging to anyone undertaking them, they are actually intended to free the person. They bring "fewness of wishes, contentment, effacement, and [the ability for] withdrawal."[42] In summary, the primary purpose of virtue is to provide physical and interior restraint and to minimize impediments to meditation.

The experience of virtue is not understood as a burden, but as an opportunity for the mind to be free from burdens. If, for example, one has a sensuous personality disposition, then a rigorously ascetical path is going to be hard at first, but only at first. The very insecurity that represents a craving mind is replaced by a kind of serenity of spirit. Buddhaghosa promises that as one grows in virtue, one becomes more alive, ever more filled with life and energy.[43]

Concentration *(Samadhi)*

Once virtue is established, Buddhaghosa next describes how the mind cultivates a spiritual posture through meditations designed for concentration. They are designed for three ends. First, they suppress and, to a degree, eliminate that which keeps the mind from being self-possessed. Traditionally, these impediments to self-possession are described as the *five hindrances* of lust, ill will, torpor, agitation/worry, and uncertainty.[44] These hindrances are the mental dispositions that interfere with both meditative concentration and insight. Second, these meditations are designed to support strengths in the psyche. For example, someone with a natural disposition toward faithfulness would do well to meditate on such things as the Buddha's qualities.[45] Such a practice would naturally draw on what is already an inherent predilection of this type of personality. Third, and conversely, some are designed to reverse unskillful mental states. For example, he recommends that a greedy or sensuous personality type would do well meditating of the foulness of the body.[46]

Types of Meditators

Buddhaghosa writes: "When a man cultivates what is unsuitable, his progress is difficult and his direct-knowledge sluggish. When he cultivates what is suitable, his progress is easy and his direct-knowledge swift. This refers to both the severing of impediments and to the object choices of meditation."[47]

This advice points us to Buddhaghosa's sections on the types of temperament. He lists six: greedy/sensuous, hating/angry, deluded/

dull, faithful, intelligent, and speculative. While he lists them as six separate personality types, each having specific sources in past habits *(karma)*, they may also be understood as only three. A faithful personality is also a greedy one, depending upon one's spiritual development. The intelligent person likewise has a parallel in anger. And the speculative is aligned with the deluded temperament. Given that each temperament has a twin, any meditation subject recommended for one temperament is also recommended for its twin.[48]

Forty Meditation Subjects

Buddhaghosa amasses quite a list of meditational subjects, forty in all, for the development of concentration.[49] Without a laborious description of them all, we see that they can be categorized in seven headings.

1. *Ten Kasinas:* These meditation subjects are visual aids intended to focus the mind in deep concentration or absorption. They include elements of earth, water, fire, and air, the colors of blue, yellow, red, and white, and the concepts of light and space. In the next section I describe how a *kasina* works.

2. *Ten Kinds of Foulness:* These are meditations of decaying corpses and are intended to provide the meditator with insight into the impermanence of things as well as an emotional distancing from sensual desire.

3. *Ten Reflections:* The first three of these are designed to inspire devotional attitudes, such as meditating on the Buddha. The next five are intended to instill in the meditator, on a fairly deep psychic level, important virtues of Buddhism, for example, generosity. And the last two are intended to bring awareness of the body and mindfulness of breathing.

4. *Four Divine-Abidings:* These meditations involve drawing up within oneself the ethos of a skillful mental state.

They are loving-kindness *(metta)*, compassion *(karuna)*, sympathetic joy *(mudita)*, and equanimity *(upekkha)*.

5. *Four Immaterial States:* These meditations are listed as consisting of boundless space, boundless consciousness, nothingness, and neither perception nor nonperception. These four meditations are really advanced levels of concentrative absorption *(jhanas)*, which are discussed in following text.[50]

6. *One Perception:* This meditation involves various ways of meditating on food consumption so as not to objectify the event of eating as that of sensual delight.

7. *One Defining:* This final meditational subject involves being able to discern a given object as one of the elements of earth, water, fire, or air. It can also include defining different experiences of the body in these terms. The purpose of this meditational strategy is to continue to divest the intellect of the delusion that the self is a solid, persisting being.

The following is an example of how a meditation brings mental absorption or *samadhi*. I will use the meditation on an earthen disk *(kasina)*.[51] One begins meditation by mental preparations, such as arousing a longing for escape from the senses. Second, one opens one's eyes moderately, looking at the disk and seeing the *sign* it represents, that is, earth. Once the object is set in the mind, the meditator, through the use of the imagination, progressively extends the scope of the mental image until the mind is sufficiently concentrated. One recognizes now that the mental hindrances are replaced with spiritual faculties: applied thought (appropriating the meditation object well), sustained thought (keeping consciousness anchored), happiness, bliss, and one-pointedness of mind. This is the first level of concentration (first *jhana*). The attainment of all higher levels of concentration is a process whereby the grosser factors of the mind are successively eliminated and subtler ones are brought into greater prominence. The meditator averts from the applied and sustained thought (second *jhana*). Then happiness is recognized as a gross factor, and so one averts from it (third *jhana*). Then bliss is recognized as impure, while equanimity and one-pointedness are seen as the real place of security (fourth *jhana*). What's happening here is that, once a meditational object is instilled in the mind, one simply releases awareness of the qualities of the mind that are progressively noticed as being less sublime.

There are four more levels of mental absorption, and these represent the *four immaterial states*, which we saw previously. Unlike the former absorptions (*jhanas*), these do not vary in compositional factors of consciousness. What is different is that the object of concentration changes. The fifth level (first *arupa-jhana*)[52] of consciousness occurs when one extends the *kasina* to the limits of one's imagination. And then to the sixth (second *arupa-jhana*), by concentrating on the space left when the *kasina* is mentally removed. The seventh (third *arupa-jhana*) is achieved when the nonexistence of boundless space becomes the object of concentration. The eighth and final level of meditation (fourth *arupa-jhana*) is called the base of neither perception nor nonperception. In focusing on the mental components of one's existence, the meditator averts to the base like a mantra *peaceful, peaceful, peaceful.* This is the highest and deepest level of concentration or *samadhi.*[53]

Experiencing Buddhist Absorption

The experience of *samadhi* practice is extraordinarily gratifying. The very nature of the *jhanas* describe the experience as the mind moves to levels of absorption that are ever more subtle and sublime. I recall being on a lengthy retreat where some of the meditators were practicing *samadhi* up to the third *jhana*. Toward the end of the retreat, their teachers had to slowly move them into insight practice (which we see in the following section), so that the shock of leaving such delightful mental states would not be so severe.

According to Buddhaghosa, *samadhi* practices are eminently important for progress. While it is possible to become attached to the experience of peace and tranquility they provide, these are the practices that allow one to come to a mental posture for insight.[54] But these meditations have two fundamental inadequacies regarding enlightenment. The first is that the purity of mind they produce is done, not by the elimination of the hindrances, but by their suppression. Of course, they also cultivate the mind in an environment that is very spiritually conducive. But in the end, the purity they produce is as temporary as any given meditation period.

The second fundamental inadequacy is that they are not curative. With exclusive use of them, one comes to a deeply happy and serene life and perhaps an extraordinary rebirth. But one cannot get off of the wheel of *samsara* through them. The situation can be likened to being in a prison cell. One can dress up the cell, making it comfortable and aesthetically pleasing. But no matter how wonderful the cell, it is still a prison. In fact, it is possible for the meditator to be so enamored by the experience of *samadhi* that these practices themselves can serve to strengthen the bars of the prison. This was the Buddha's critique of Hinduism. The only way to escape the prison of *samsara* is through insight.

Understanding *(Panna)* or Insight *(Vipassana)*

We have seen that concentration practices *(samadhi)* cannot bring one to *Nirvana*. They do not have the capacity for seeing reality for what it is *(anicca, anatta,* and *dukkha)* and in fact suppress this knowledge for the sake of concentration. Their intention is either to quiet or cultivate the mind; it is not to know it. Insight into the characteristics of the self (and by extension, the world) as impermanent, selfless, and dissatisfying is the knowledge that liberates. Buddhaghosa writes that true knowledge is not merely perception, but "penetration of the characteristics as impermanent, painful, and not-self."[55]

If the three sections of *The Path of Purification* are understood to reflect liberative progression, then we see that the first stage is to embrace virtue, the second stage is to train the mind through concentration and skillful mental dispositions, and the third stage is to understand reality for what it is *(panna)*. Because of its importance, Buddhaghosa devotes nearly half of *The Path of Purification* to understanding.

It would be laborious for us to detail every step of insight meditation *(vipassana)*, and, I think, unnecessary. But perhaps a brief outline is in order, for the meditator practicing *vipassana* does go through a series of levels of insight. Each series is but a deeper penetration of self-understanding into the three qualities of all existence. It is this understanding that allows one to be liberated from the *karma* produced by desire.[56]

Buddhaghosa suggests that the first experience of deep insight comes through meditating on the aggregates that comprise the person. One discerns proper impersonal elements and recognizes the self to be nonconstitutive *(anatta)*.[57] Here in meditation one may perhaps watch one's breath or analyze the energy flow through the body. Experiences arise and dissipate, and one realizes that there is no essential self behind them. The second purification occurs when one perceives through bare attention how the *karma* process works. In this purification, one literally sees how desire creates the conditions for the furtherance of the aggregates.[58] Again, the practice is through watching and analyzing. One sees, through bare attention, how one's mind tends to incline to pleasant experiences and avert from unpleasant ones. Practicing equanimity, one neither clings to nor avoids these experiences. Instead, one watches how the mind tends to incline toward or away from them. In the third stage of progress, one understands how impermanence *(anicca)* is painful and afflictive.[59] This is the result of watching the inner drama of how one reacts to the rise and fall of these impersonal experiences. The next meditative stage involves the culmination of insight. The aggregates are more profoundly viewed as impermanent, and the meditator is utterly focused on the dissolution of all mental and physical arisings. One realizes that arising is suffering, non-arising is bliss. There comes an intense desire for liberation in *Nirvana*.[60] The final stage of insight leading to total liberation is a change-of-lineage-knowledge whereby the cycle of rebirth has been broken. There are four different states here, each referring to an ever more subtle breakdown of the lingering habits of desire and clinging.[61]

The three levels of purification ought to be understood as progressive, with stages within each one. Without moral restraint, the mind is too distracted for deep meditation. It is the foundation of all further work. Furthermore, we have noted that deep concentration leads to a kind of cultured mind that is conducive to understanding. One cannot have liberating insight without trained attention.[62] But as we saw, *samadhi* by itself does not lead to liberation, and could even reinforce one's attachments. What it does is to provide support for insight practice *(vipassana)*.

Perhaps, however, the path can also be understood as all three purifications mutually developing with and reinforcing each other.[63] Mental restraint is virtually impossible without the mental cultivation found in concentration, or more important, in insight practice. Further, as one comes to greater insight into the nature of the clinging mind, one becomes even more morally virtuous, rejecting subtler forms of greed and attachments. This freedom of mind allows for even deeper levels of concentration. In short, all three practices tend to mutually cultivate and support each other.

Spiritual Paths Compared

Convergences

Ascetical Project

Both John of the Cross and Buddhaghosa describe the initial stage to spiritual liberation as beginning with asceticism. This is the foundation for any real advancement. John describes these as the active night of the senses. The object of the active night is to minimize sensual gratifications and to wean the soul from pursuing God for the often-unconscious reason of self-gratification. For Buddhaghosa, the ascetical exercises also are intended to wean the mind from its acquisitive propensities. Both describe to varying degrees how challenging this may be initially. But, for both, the purpose of asceticism is actually quite positive; it frees the soul from the very things that disturbs it. We think we want gratifications in order to comfort the soul, but in more incisive investigation we find that they actually do the opposite. They make us restless and insecure.

Detachment

A second obvious convergence between these two paths is the emphasis on detachment. I mentioned this in the previous chapter on anthropology, since it so intimately parallels the central problem of the unreformed spiritual person. Both John and Buddhaghosa describe a path that progressively and systematically brings one to radical detachment. John describes this as a moral issue, a matter of the will. Buddhists call this posture of detachment *equanimity*, and John would agree. "True love," he writes, "receives all things from the beloved—prosperity, adversity, even chastisement—with the same evenness of soul, since they are his will."[64] So important is this equanimity that he even recommends the soul's inclining to the least gratifying in all things as the safer route. But it doesn't stop with our experience of natural gratifications. Even supernatural experiences of God require detachment. The soul can even become addicted to these.[65] Buddhaghosa agrees. One can become attached especially to gratifying meditational experiences.

The role of detachment for Buddhaghosa is utterly tied to his presentation of dependent-origination. The *karma* process has everything to do with the will's grasping. Volition depends upon clinging, and clinging only arises from craving. When craving is broken, *karma* ceases.[66] Insight practice *(vipassana)*, which allows for the breaking of *karma*, requires a meditative posture of complete detachment. Recall that the mind comes to see clearly only when greed and aversion no longer dominate the mind's reactions.

Deconstruction of Both Self and Experience

We saw in the preceding chapter that John and Buddhaghosa have radically different understandings of the nature of the human being. But there is a fascinating convergence in the experience of spiritual progress with regard to the self. One's sense of self gets deconstructed, and all of its experiences are relativized. For John, the greatest final attachment for the soul is that of spiritual experience. God's graces were experienced as sublime, energizing, and the completion of the soul. The dark night of the spirit forces the soul to confront even this as an attachment—even the desire to be loved by God—so that the soul can live ultimately only for God. This emptying of the spiritual faculties allows for God to transform the soul. For him, the deconstruction of the self is annihilation of self-identity based on the narcissistic appropriation of experience. The soul, while realizing its human status, identifies with God's will, God's wisdom, and God's universal love. It can only do this when it loses itself in God.

Buddhaghosa also describes late stage practice in similar veins. Each of the five stages in advanced *vipassana* practice is described as progressively subtler confrontations with attachments. One comes to ever-deeper understandings of one's own impermanence and selflessness. It is in late stage practice where the meditator sees that there is no self and nothing possible to cling to whereby one comes to true liberative knowledge.[67]

diesel fuel   381. 30   87.70

petrol motor

Divergences

Different Meditative Strategies

While both paths describe a meditative/contemplative agenda that proceeds from the more exterior to the more interior parts of the self, and while both intend to bring the aspirant to increasing levels of detachment, they are not at all the same. The differences in the paths can be analyzed by differences in the way one is drawn into the path and the way different parts of the path relate to each other.

The first clue that the meditative dynamics are not the same can be observed by attending to John's three criteria as to whether one is being drawn into contemplative prayer. The soul is drawn to a more intimate knowledge of God, and thus the use of the imagination in prayer is experienced as utterly frustrating. John warns that all the signs need to be present for contemplative prayer or the soul will surely regress. When we compare his advice to what we see in *The Path of Purification,* we may legitimately pause. Theravada Buddhist practices are for anyone with a moderately balanced psyche. Even children are taught these practices. My point here is simply that the form of meditative detachment that John teaches is a different form, not only in name but in substance, from that of Buddhaghosa. It is a form that replaces former meditative modalities, and must be engaged in only by divine initiative.

The second clue that these may be really quite different paths can be seen in their respective strategies, and in the relationship that meditative practices have with more contemplative postures. For John, once the soul experiences these signs that it is being led into contemplative prayer, then the use of the imagination in prayer (mental prayer) acts as an impediment to progress.[68] The path of Saint John of the Cross is a path toward a deeper intimacy with God. Such intimacy requires abandoning mediated and indirect ways for an unmediated, direct encounter. It is not for everyone, but is undertaken only by divine invitation. This is strikingly different in Buddhist meditation, whereby both tracks of meditation should be used throughout one's development. There is no time when the aspirant cannot do either track of meditation, nor does one meditational form impede the other. One may practice a devotional meditation, such as meditating on the Buddha, one day and practice *vipassana* the next. In fact, they mutually reinforce each other. Even in a given meditative sitting, one may begin developing *samadhi* and move to insight methodology analyzing the *jhana* levels for the three characteristics.

Nature of the Practice

An important difference between these two paths is the very nature of their meditative practices. John's description of contemplative prayer has as striking resonance with both tracks of Buddhist meditation. But on closer scrutiny, it corresponds to neither of them. What he describes is highly concentrative and often blissful. Just looking at stanzas 5–8 of his poem *The Dark Night* tells us much:

> O guiding light!
> O night more lovely than the dawn!
> O night that has united
> The Lover with his beloved,
> Transforming the beloved in her lover.

> Upon my flowering breast
> Which I kept wholly for him alone,
> There he lay sleeping,
> And I caressing him
> There in a breeze from the fanning cedars.

> When the breeze blew from the turret,
> As I parted his hair,
> It wounded my neck with its gentle hand,
> Suspending all my senses.

I abandoned and forgot myself,
Laying my face on my Beloved;
All things ceased; I went out from myself,
Leaving my cares
Forgotten among the lilies.

These lines—"Suspending all my senses...All things ceased; I went out from myself"—sound similar to *samadhi* practices whereby the concentrative project suppresses from the mind all thoughts and feelings, and focuses the mind only on the object of meditation. Further, John describes something highly affective: "O night more lovely than the dawn!/O night that has united/Lover with his beloved." It is *samadhi* practice that can be described as gratifying, in the sense that some of the *jhanas* are defined by their qualities of bliss, happiness, and so on.

On the other hand, it could be argued that what John is really describing is better likened to *vipassana* practice. After all, they both share the essential posture of detachment and openness to whatever may come. One allows reality to be or do as it will, with no expectations. It requires a kind of death to the self, as it were. And one could argue that the void of detachment means that ultimacy (whether understood as God or God *Nirvana*) would fill that void. All we have to do is be detached and grace will come. Then it seems logical that Christian contemplation and Buddhist *vipassana* are essentially the same, or at least will do the same to the soul.

Both interpretations, I believe, fail to actually look at what is being taught. John's contemplation is a union of love, a meeting of lovers. While it shares with *vipassana* the demand to be utterly detached, it has only one intention: intimacy with God. Such an intimacy *(noticia amarosa)* can be recognized and differentiated from other experiences as the meditator progresses in the stage of proficiency.[69] *Vipassana* practice, while it is detached, also has an agenda. It intends to deconstruct the self by way of noticing the arisings of aggregate formations and the dynamics of *karma*. It is

71

a meditative strategy of investigating and watching the disturbing truths of Buddhists ontology—*anicca*, *anatta*, and *dukkha*. From the perspective of Buddhism, any meeting between God and the soul would cultivate the very opposite agenda.

Love

While both paths describe similarities in the aspirant's growth in joy and freedom, there is a central quality in the experience of the path that radically differentiates them. This is the experience of love. Love is not absent in Buddhism. In *The Path of Purification* one may grow in love as one practices the divine-abidings meditations. Each meditation can legitimately be described as different aspects of love. Loving-kindness *(metta)* desires good for others; compassion *(karuna)* is love that inclines toward easing suffering; sympathetic joy *(mudita)* is love inclined toward other's experience of happiness; and equanimity *(upekkha)* is love's insistence on non-enmeshment so that one loves the other as other and not as an attachment to self. So there really is love in Buddhist spirituality. But this love has only conventional value; it has no ultimate reference.[70] *Nirvana*, being a *supramundane* reality, has nothing ultimately to do with them. The divine-abidings meditations are meant to balance *vipassana* practice. They soften the heart and give one greater meditative pliancy. They are also meant to help one grow in right relationships. But they do not describe anything of ultimate value in Buddhaghosa's path.

When we compare this with John's contemplative agenda, we see quite a striking difference. Love takes on absolute importance. It is God's love that is communicated to the soul, God's love as the agent of the soul's transformation, and God's love as the soul's ultimate end. Even before union with God the soul can literally be absorbed in love. And the soul can feel such clarity in these experiences, John says, that it can intuit God's universal love literally drenching the universe.[71]

In chapter 1, I related a statement from William James's famous *The Varieties of Religious Experience*. In it James argues that beneath the variety of articulations of mysticism in each religion lies the very same experience. This belief is rampant among many in comparative religion. What we see in comparing John's and Buddhaghosa's respective mystical paths is that such alignment would have to dismiss their foundational beliefs, their paths, and their expressed experience. John's is a mysticism of love, while Buddhaghosa's is one of deep, penetrating, impersonal insight. In this regard, they cannot be farther apart.

Notes

1. Saint John's path is not strictly linear. Regularly he uses the term *ordinariamente* to speak about how souls experience their spiritual lives or ought to go about interpreting experience. He recognized that people have different needs and dispositions with regard to their spiritual lives and that this must be reverenced (*Ascent* I.13.1; *Dark Night* I.14.4–6). A running dictum that he employs is that ultimately God is gentle and that God only leads according to our unique dispositions and potentials. So the spiritual path, even as he outlines it in a delineated and progressive way, is understood as unique in each individual. See also *Ascent* II.17.2; III.39.1; *Dark Night* I.2.6; *Living Flame* 3.59.

2. *Ascent* Pro.3–7.

3. *Ascent* Pro.9.

4. "This doctrine is itself good and very necessary" (*Ascent* Pro.8). John did believe that his spirituality points to a universal goal, that is, union with God. Though few people reach this in their lives, God's will is that all would reach it. God, however, "finds few vessels that will endure so lofty and sublime work" (*Living Flame* 2.27).

5. *Dark Night* I.6.6.

6. *Ascent* III.29.2; *Dark Night* I.1.3.

7. *Ascent* II.14.4; II.16.11; II.17.5.

8. *Dark Night* I.2.1–8.

9. *Ascent* I.13.3–9. We saw that the appetites in themselves are natural and necessary to human beings. The asceticism of the appetites, which John recommends, primarily refers to *disordered* appetites. He explains this in *Ascent* I.3. But this is not entirely the case. His advice in chapter 13 is of a broader asceticism. His agenda is for one to minimize one's pleasurable sensory experiences and create a kind of sensual vacuum. He suggests that the soul become inclined toward the most difficulty, the most distasteful, least pleasant, least consoling, and so on. This is not asceticism for asceticism's sake, however. Clearly it is for the primary purpose of shaking off the stranglehold that our attachments have. For more clarification, see *Ascent* I.4.1; II.7.7. I believe that it has a secondary purpose too. Such a minimization of pleasurable experience tends to center the soul for contemplative prayer. Sensory overload, even if one is detached, is very disturbing for deep contemplation. See also Alain Cugno,

St. John of the Cross: Reflections on Mystical Experiences, trans. Wall (New York: Seabury Press, 1982), 50–71.

10. *Dark Night* I.8.3; I.9.4.

11. *Dark Night* I.9.4.

12. *Ascent* II.13.2–4; *Dark Night* I.9.2–8.

13. *Dark Night* I.9.3ff.

14. See *Ascent* II.13.7; II.14.8; *Dark Night* I.1.2.

15. *Dark Night* I.8.2; I.9.4–6.

16. *Dark Night* II.1.1. Clearly, during this phase, one is encouraged to leave meditations behind so as to more fully enter the contemplative process. Proficients have moved from a meditative (discursive and imaginative) prayer form to one that is contemplative (nonconceptual without the use of the imagination). This is not absolute, however. Some discursive mediation and use of images, especially initially, are acceptable and even helpful (*Ascent* II.14.1; II.15.1–2; III.39.1).

17. *Ascent* II.26.5–9; II.32.2–4.

18. *Ascent* II.13.7; II.15.1–5; *Dark Night* I.9.3–6; I.10.4–6; I.11.1–2.

19. Ascent II.24.4; II.26.5–10; II.32.2–4; *Dark Night* II.24.3; *Spiritual Canticle* 14–15.14–16.

20. *Ascent* III.2.4–13.

21. *Dark Night* II.16.1.

22. *Dark Night* II.7.4.

23. *Dark Night* II.5.2–3; II.9.10–11; II.12.1–4; II.13.10.

24. *Spiritual Canticle* 14–15.14.

25. *Living Flame* 3.33. One of the traps of more contemplative methods of prayer is what has been termed *sinking mind*. In this state, one prays in a warm, fuzzy, dreamy state and can be deluded into thinking that this is what spiritual masters mean by the faculties being "put to sleep." Clearly, in the contemplation taught by John of the Cross, the mind is highly alert and focused. See, for example, *Ascent* II.14.6. The posture of the soul is that of an active and intense hungering of the intellect and yearning of the memory and will for God (*Living Flame* 3.20–21).

26. *Ascent* I.1.3.

27. *Dark Night* II.2.1.

28. See, for example, *Dark Night* I.1.1.

29. *Dark Night* II.1.1–2; II.5–7; *Living Flame* 1.19–23. For an interesting study on Merton's understanding of the false and true self, see Anne

Carr, *A Search for Wisdom and Spirit: Thomas Merton's Theology of Self* (Notre Dame, IN: Notre Dame Press, 1988).

30. *Ascent* I.1.3.

31. *Dark Night* II.5.5; II.9.8–9; II.11.7.

32. *Living Flame* 3.33.

33. *Living Flame* 2.23.

34. *Living Flame* 2.8.

35. Recall the Buddha's silence about *supramundane* realities.

36. *The Path of Purification*, 1.1.

37. *Path*, 1.7.

38. Buddhaghosa writes that it is "the necessary condition" (*Path* 1.11). See also Edmond Peret, *"Voies de contemplation dans Bouddisme Theravada,"* in *Meditation dans le Christianisme et les autres religions*, ed. Dhavamony (Rome: Gregorian University Press, 1976), 67.

39. Peret, 6.

40. Buddhaghosa does mention the five precepts, but these are interiorized on a much more sensitive level. For example, the precept of having a *right livelihood* is usually meant some occupation that does not harm another. But in *The Path of Purification* it includes how a monk thinks about the few things he owns, such as how he receives and estimates his clothing or the food that he begs, even examining this latter bite by bite.

41. *Path*, 2.12.

42. *Path*, 2.78–2.83.

43. *Path*, 2.1; 2.83.

44. *Path*, 4.104.

45. *Path*, 3.102.

46. *Path*, 3.121.

47. *Path*, 3.116.

48. *Path*, 3.75–3.80.

49. *Path*, 3.104ff.

50. I am following Gunaratana here. In his doctoral dissertation he demonstrates that, while Buddhaghosa places the *Immaterial States* as four of the forty meditative subjects, they really belong to Buddhaghosa's description of the *jhanas* under the heading *arupa-jhana*, since they are advancements in concentration from the four initial *jhanas*. See Henepola Gunaratana, *The Path of Serenity and Insight: An Explanation of Buddhist Jhanas* (Delhi: Motilal Benarsidass, 1985). See also Winston King,

Theravada Meditation: The Buddhist Transformation of Yoga (University Park: Pennsylvania State University Press, 1980), 52ff.

51. The term *kasina* etymologically means "whole," and it is used in the sense that this type of meditation unifies the mind completely.

52. *Arupa* is a term that means "immaterial."

53. The Theravadin tradition also knows a meditative level deeper than the above, referred to as *nirodha* (cessation), but Buddhaghosa does not include this.

54. *Path*, 12.1.

55. *Path*, 14.3.

56. The Buddha's *Satipatthana sutta* is central here. This is his teaching on the Four Foundations of Mindfulness. Modern commentator Thera Nyanaponika, in summing up the role of *satipatthana*, describes it thusly: "All the Buddha's methods ultimately converge in the way of mindfulness." See *The Heart of Buddhist Meditation* (York Beach, ME: Samuel Weiser, 1965), 7.

57. This is *purification of view* (chap. 18). One sees in the aggregates the four elements of the universe, that is, earth, wind, fire, and ether.

58. This is *purification of overcoming doubt* (chap. 19). Here one sees that the pleasure or pain that arises does not last. That is, that the meditator is brought to the point where, without clinging to experience, feelings of pleasure and pain are allowed simply to be, arising and falling without any clinging.

59. This is *purification by knowledge and vision of what is the path and what is not the path* (chap. 20).

60. This is *purification by knowledge and vision of the way* (chap. 21). The great desire for liberation comes when one painfully realizes that there is no refuge in phenomenal reality in which to hide. Because of this, formations that do arise can be terrifying, since one is aware that there is nothing to cling to and no refuge for security. This is really a protracted three-step stage. One experiences the *knowledge of reflection:* clarity regarding the characteristics of all of life; *knowledge of equanimity about formations:* both terror and delight drops off and one has equanimity as to their arisings and dissipations; and *conformity knowledge:* one realizes that the path will arise before one (21.29).

61. This is *purification by knowledge and vision* (chap. 22). There are four levels here. The first is called *stream-entry*, whereby if one did not progress further there would be at most seven rebirths. The second level

is called the *once-returner*, who is guaranteed only one more rebirth without further progress. The third level of development in this state is that of a *non-returner*, who may be reborn once, but it is assured that this would be in a blissful realm. The final level is that of a Buddhist saint, the *arahant*. Buddhaghosa says that the *arahant* has both serenity (associated with *samadhi*) and insight powers in perfect harmony. The differences among these noble states are not great, but refer to very subtle distinctions in psychic predilections to desire. Buddhaghosa believes that one could progress through each of these levels quickly, even in one sitting (22.20).

62. For an excellent presentation on this, see Gunaratana, 199ff.

63. Bhikkhu Bodhi describes it this way: "Morality restrains the defilements in their coarsest form, their outflow in unwholesome actions; concentration removes their more refined manifestations in distractive and restless thoughts; wisdom eradicates their subtle, latent tendencies by penetrating with direct insight." See his Introduction to Nyanaponika's *The Vision of Dhamma* (London: Rider, 1986), xxi. See also Peret, 69.

64. *Spiritual Canticle* 11.10.

65. *Ascent* II.10.

66. *Path*, 17.292.

67. Specifically the consciousness aggregate.

68. Recall the discussion in chapter 2. In fact, the early proficient may be allowed some periods of meditative prayer, but only as one is being weaned off of them (*Ascent* II.14.1). They should decrease, if they are allowed at all, while one focuses exclusively on a more nondiscursive loving communion with God.

69. Much of *The Ascent of Mount Carmel* is spent on describing how the soul often does not know what is happening spiritually, and therefore must trust God. The careful reader, however, will notice that such teaching forms John's critique of why noncontemplative experiences must not be trusted, and why one must be detached from them. We must recall that the intent of *The Ascent* is to lead aspirants in the active nights of the senses and spirit. This type of critique of spiritual experience does not exist in the same way in *Dark Night*, which describes the passive nights, those dominated by sheer grace. In the passive nights, the soul often does recognize God's activity. This recognition comes by the soul's experience of divine love or wisdom, or by the experience of divine purification.

70. These meditations are called divine-abiding *(brahma-viharas)* because they correspond to rebirth levels in Buddhist cosmology (realms

of the gods). When they are practiced intensely, one may expect rebirth there. But such promises are also made regarding intensive meditational practice on, for example, the immaterial states *(arupa-jhanas)*. These latter states correspond to even higher levels of Buddhist cosmology, and thus, represent higher rebirths. In either case, such practices and their corresponding cosmological levels are still only *mundane* and have nothing to do with *Nirvana*.

71. See *Ascent* II.24.4; II.26.5–10; II.32.2–4; *Dark Night* II.24.3; *Spiritual Canticle* 14–15.14–16; *Living Flame* 2.10.

Chapter Four

Final Bliss

What Are We Striving For?

Many Christians, if asked about the ultimate goal of faith, would naturally say that it was going to heaven. And of course, this would surely be right. Traditionally, Catholics phrased it: "We were made to love and serve God in this world and to enjoy him in the next." It does beg the question, however: What is heaven? What do we mean by this term? If going to heaven is looked at as a personal reward, as some kind of self-possession, then we have an ironic problem. For it is this very idea of the self that needs to be let go.

We see this problem raised as in Jesus' own words: "If anyone wants to be a follower of mine, let him renounce himself and take up his cross every day and follow me. Anyone who wants to save his life will lose it; but anyone who loses his life for my sake, will save it" (Luke 9:23–24). Obviously, Jesus speaks here paradoxically. But he is referring to a spiritual dynamic that is quite real. This self that needs to be renounced or lost is the narcissistic self, one that sees its own interests as if the center of its own universe.

There is a Hindu story of a holy woman who went into a town square with a large bowl. She sat by the market putting dirt into the bowl and a little water, and she stirred. This drew some attention of a few passersby. But what really caught the attention of many was that periodically she would put her hand into the bowl and pull out a gold nugget. When she had enough gold to finance her continued journey, she got up to leave. A merchant seized the opportunity and ran over to her.

"Are you a magician?"

"No," she replied.

"Is this a magic bowl?"

"No," she said, "it's just an ordinary bowl."

He asked her to explain how she got the gold to come out. "All I do," she said, "is put in ordinary dirt, add ordinary water, and then stir. Then sometimes a gold nugget emerges. There's no magic here." He was not convinced, and ended up buying the bowl for quite a sum. She gave this money to the local orphanage and continued her journey. The merchant was delighted, and for many days he did as she had instructed. But he found no gold no matter how hard or long he tried. Several months later, the woman was passing through the same town and he accosted her. "You tricked me," he said. "I did everything you said, but I found no gold." She answered, "Oh, there is one thing I did neglect to tell you. In order to get the gold, you have to renounce your greed."

Do I love God in order to get something out of him? Is this real love or just another expression of the egotistical self? Here is the problem, the paradox. In order to attain to the very beatitude we were created for, we have to renounce the ego's very interest in it, *as if it were a possession for the self.* Denying oneself and living only for God means that there is nothing for the self to be attached to, to seek, or to advance as its own. At the core, we only make sense in God. Our only attachment is God himself, our only seeking is God's glory, and the only thing we ought to legitimately advance is God's kingdom. In the abstract, this makes sense to most Christians, but to actually live such a profound reality, there must be a kind of *paschal dying* to ourselves. Saint John of the Cross speaks of this kind of paradoxical self-denial in his famous sketch of the ascent of Mount Carmel, the peak representing union with God: "Only the honor and glory of God dwells on this mount."

For John, the full realization of this paschal death to the self can only come from grace in the passive night of the spirit. In a very real way, we are emptied, even of ourselves, and (ironically) even as the full flowering of our true selves emerges mysteriously in God. In perhaps his most mature book, *New Seeds of Contemplation*, Thomas Merton describes the paradox we are discussing. Collectively, the following medley of citations brings us deeper into the mystery:

> The secret of my full identity is hidden in God....To say that I am made in the image of God is to say that love is the reason for my existence, for God is love. Love is my true identity. Selflessness is my true self. Love is my true character, Love is my name....[One] lives in emptiness and freedom, as if one had no longer a limited and exclusive *self* that distinguished oneself from God and other people....What happens is that the separate identity that is *you* apparently disappears and nothing seems to be left but a pure freedom indistinguishable from the infinite Freedom, love identified with Love....God is the *I* who acts there. God is the one Who loves and knows and rejoices.[1]

So what is left? God and his grace is what is left, and this turns out to be concomitant with our deepest self. This is what union of God is for John, and is in fact the traditional teaching throughout Christianity. In the *Catechism of the Catholic Church* we read, "By participation of the Spirit, we become communicants in the divine nature....For this reason, those in whom the Spirit dwells are divinized....The purpose of the Incarnation is that humanity might become divine....Grace makes us partakers of the divine nature....Grace deifies us."[2] For the Christian, heaven is not simply living with God or enjoying God, but actually living one's life with and in him. Thus, our understanding of ourselves as self-seeking or separate from God is an appropriation of the self in actual contrast to the divine life we are meant to have.

John teaches that this divinizing union with God, which we hope for in heaven, can also be experienced in this life to a large degree. So similar is this experience of union here and now with heaven, that John says nothing but a thin veil separates one from God and from the final beatitude. Buddhists also understand that the life we have now, if it is enlightened, is like the final end. We have used the term *Nirvana* to note that ultimate purpose in this life. One has entered or realized *Nirvana* once one has broken the chains of *karma*. One still continues on in life, but it is a radically changed life. Once an enlightened person dies, one is said to enter *Pari-Nirvana (final-Nirvana)*. So in each respective path, the final end or ultimate destiny of the self can be in many respects already known here on earth.

We could also answer the question about the ultimate aim for Christian faith by saying that it is to become a saint, that is, one totally sanctified by grace. We become perfect as God is perfect (Matt 5:48), compassionate as God is compassionate (Luke 6:36), or dare we say it, holy as God is holy (Lev 11:45). Surely we only know the fullness of this reality in the beatific vision, but we can know radical sanctity here and now also. For Buddhists a saint is an *arahat*, someone fully enlightened, who has entered *Nirvana* and lives this lifetime fully liberated. Such holiness in this life, from both Christian and Buddhist perspectives, is what this chapter addresses. They represent the ultimate horizons of the life of faith.

Saint John of the Cross and Union with God

The highest stage in John's contemplative progression is this stage of union with God, which he also calls *spiritual marriage*. Union with God is nothing less than the divinization of the soul through participation in the divine life. This state is neither static nor one of perpetual absorption.[3] He describes it like this: "The faculties are not always in actual union, but the substance of the soul is perpetually so."[4] It is the "condition of Adam's state of innocence" in which the whole person is in harmony with God and creation.[5] The nature of union with God is most fully described in *The Spiritual Canticle* and *The Living Flame of Love*. In the beginning of *The Ascent of Mount Carmel*, John writes, "Love produces equality and likeness."[6] This dictum is especially telling of what the dynamic of union with God at the end of one's spiritual journey. The soul is transformed into the Beloved. It is a total possession of God who totally possesses the soul.[7]

The quality of transformation that John describes can hardly know a superlative. He says that all things of both God and the soul become one. In terms of our natures, they are still as distinct as creature from Creator or as a being from Being itself. But by participation in the divine life, the soul is made divine *relationally*.[8] John offers two strikingly beautiful descriptions of this newfound love between the soul and God, the first using the metaphor of fire. He says that the flames of love, which the soul had known to be the transforming power of God, are now a mutual flame, indistinguishable from each other. They originate neither from the Holy Spirit nor from the soul alone. Rather, they arise from them both. That God's love would be experienced by the soul as having a mutual source is, he teaches, the soul's splendor and glorification.[9]

A second description he offers can be found in a song he imagines God singing to the soul: "I am yours and for you and delighted to be what I am so as to be yours and give myself to you."[10] This, he says, is God's ultimate illustration of supreme humility and esteem for the soul; that it pleases God to make the soul his equal by this *exchange of selves*.[11]

Since the soul is transformed by participation in the divine life and actually lives God's divine life on earth, John teaches that all the acts of the soul become divine as well, since the Holy Spirit makes them all. Thus the intellect, the memory, and the will become as though God's.[12] The divinization of the will in love takes principal importance. The soul is said to love as God loves and even love within the Trinity's own interrelational love.[13] In summary, in unitive participation with God, the soul finds its will so transformed that it loves as God loves.

The soul also knows as God knows. We must recall, however, that this kind of knowing is not in terms of knowing information. We recall that the spiritual faculties are made for the created world and have the limitations that correspond to the natural world. These limitations are always part of our psyches. As we have seen, however, these faculties do have the ability to be engaged *supernaturally* through infused grace. In fact, his whole contemplative agenda is based on letting go of the natural use of these faculties in faith, hope, and love. Thus, knowledge of God is a *dark wisdom*. The soul is aware that it knows the mystery of God, but one cannot communicate this in objective terms even to oneself. It is not *things* that we know, but *God* whom we know. And God is supreme mystery to the intellect. Even when John describes the nature of an *intellectual vision*, that is, direct communication by God of some divine mystery, such as the Trinity, the soul cannot communicate this knowledge to its intellect in a rational way. All that is communicated to the soul dwells in a kind of mystery. John asserts that, since this communication is pure contemplation, the soul clearly understands that it is ineffable.[14]

Buddhism and *Nirvana*

In chapter 2 we looked at Buddhist anthropology, and particularly that there is no essential self. We saw that this doctrine is understood by Theravada Buddhists as absolutely valid and true. Yet it is only true insofar as it relates to phenomenal reality. Doctrine has two uses for Buddhists. First, it describes reality as it is experienced on *this side of Nirvana*. Second, and even more important, it has an instrumental use.[15] Buddhist doctrines should be strictly read within their liberating agenda. This pragmatic approach follows the Buddha's self-described purpose for teaching. In the *Cula-Malunkyaputta Sutta*, a disciple asked the Buddha ten well-known, classical metaphysical questions, such as whether the universe is eternal or whether the Buddha exists after death.

The Buddha likened such questions to a person being shot by a poisoned arrow and before having it removed it absurdly demands to know all about the arrow, bow, and archer. The Buddha rhetorically asked his disciple why he had never taught these things. "Because it is not useful, it is not fundamentally connected with the spiritual holy life, it is not conducive to detachment, cessation, tranquility, deep penetration, full realization, *Nirvana*. This is why I have not told you about them."[16]

Likewise, Buddhaghosa only devotes one small section in *The Path of Purification* to the direct discussion of *Nirvana*. *Nirvana* itself is an enigmatic word. It literally means "to blow out." It would be a term used to describe the extinguishing of a candle, for example. According to the Four Noble Truths, what is on fire is desire or thirst in the mind. It is this desire that causes the experience of life to be *dukkha* and feeds the continuous rounds of rebirth. Fundamental to Buddhaghosa's brief discussion is his refutation of the claim that *Nirvana* is simply a term to describe the annihilation of the self, and that otherwise it does not have a reference. Buddhaghosa roundly rejects this nihilistic interpretation by insisting that *Nirvana* is something very real.[17]

The problem of describing *Nirvana* is that it is a *supramundane* reality. And, thus, not subject to the rules of other realities.[18] More often Buddhaghosa describes *Nirvana* negatively, for what it is not. It is uncaused, unformed, measureless, and signless.[19] While it is a reality of permanence to seek, it cannot be entered into or produced through meditation. Rather, it arises on its own.[20] In this sense, all one can do is avail oneself to *Nirvana*. It is both a void as well as something that can be realized.[21] Because it is described also as extinction and cessation, Buddhaghosa assures his readers that it has actual existence and that it can be apprehended.[22]

Here we see that any positive description of its existence metaphysically violates its true essence. There exists a saying that those who know about *Nirvana* say nothing, while those who speak of it betray their ignorance. In this sense, *Nirvana* has no *analogy of being*. For many theists, even though God is beyond objectification, we can speak of God rightly even if in a limited way. By analogy we can say that "God is love" or "God is good." It says something true about God, even if God is beyond all conceptualization. There is no such possibility with *Nirvana*. It has no correlative in the created world.[23]

If *Nirvana* cannot be described by what it is positively, Buddhaghosa does describe what it means to have realized it. It is defined by the opposite qualities of those plaguing the mind prior to enlightenment. That is, it has the qualities of non-greed, non-hate, and non-delusion.[24] Quite probably he describes it negatively in order to avoid speculations about it. In the beginning of *The Path of Purification*, he says that *Nirvana* is the same as purification, whereby one becomes devoid of all stains and is utterly pure.[25] Having realized *Nirvana* then, and because *karma* has been stopped, there is a cessation or non-arising of formations for the self. This means first, that at the point of death there will be nothing for rebirth-linking. It is at death that one is said to enter *Pari-Nirvana* (final blowing-out). For a Buddhist saint *(arahat)*, however, this cessation refers to the non-arising of desire here and now.

In the *Majjhima Nikayha*, the Buddha illustrates the enigmatic quality of *Pari-Nirvana* in his conversation with his disciple Vaccha:

"If a fire were blazing in front of you, Vaccha, would you know that it was [present]?"

"Yes, good Gotama."

"And would you know the reason for its blazing?"

"Yes, because it had a supply of grass and sticks."

"And would you know if it were to be put out *(nirvana-yeyya)?*"

"Yes, good Gotama."

"And on its being put out, would you know the direction the fire had gone from here—east, west, north, south?"

"This question does not apply, good Gotama. For the fire blazed because it had a supply of grass and sticks, but when it had consumed this and had no other fuel, then being without fuel, it is reckoned as gone out."

"Even so, Vaccha, the material shape, that feeling, perception, those impulses, that consciousness by which one, in defining the Tathagata [Buddha himself], might define him [the aggregates]—all that have been got rid of by the Tathagata, cut off at the root, made like a palm tree stump that can come to no further existence in the future. Freed from reckoning by material shape, feeling, perception, the impulses, consciousness is the Tathagata; he is deep, immeasurable, unfathomable as is the ocean. 'Arises' does not apply, nor does 'does not arise,' nor 'both arises and does not arise,' nor 'neither arises nor does not arise.'"[26]

Ultimate Horizons Compared

Convergences: Living in Wisdom and Freedom

As we have seen, Buddhaghosa does not describe *Nirvana* positively, but rather in terms of the removal of those qualities of greed, hated, and delusion, which ravage the mind. It is the state of existence without those qualities. One exists in *Nirvana* with utter purity of mind and heart. Two concepts describe the nature of this purity: peace and freedom. Nothing disturbs the mind, now that all clinging is gone. And since the mind is utterly nonreactive and nongrasping, it lives in absolute freedom. Recall that I described the liberated mind as now free from volitions. This does not mean that the *arahat* does not intend things, but rather that, since there is no narcissistic desire, it is as though wisdom itself were working through the *arahat*'s mind. He or she simply acts compassionately, spiritually skillfully, wisely, and perfectly. And one does so because all impediments to such compassion and wisdom are forever removed. This freedom should not be seen as having free choices, as if between good and evil. For the *arahat*, the difference between choosing a skillful compassionate act or an unskillful narcissistic act is no choice at all. It is above all a freedom that suggests complete unification of truth.

This same dynamic is found in John's description of union. The soul becomes one with God through love. Like Buddhaghosa, John describes the saint as being in perfect peace. The soul has found its true end. It seeks nothing else and is in perfect harmony with God, with oneself, and with the created world. Further, like the *arahat*, John's saint has perfect freedom. This too is not a freedom of choices, but a freedom that arises from being aligned with God's perfect freedom.

As Buddhaghosa describes an *arahat* living as though wisdom itself were acting through one, John says the same. It is God now who acts through the soul, it is as if the Holy Spirit was performing one's actions personally.[27] This does not exactly mean that the soul is passive or not longer acting. It is, rather, that the soul knows its perfect freedom and the full flowering of the self in and through God. Operatively, the soul is simply not different from God. When the will of the soul is united to God's will, there are no questions of choosing between better or lesser, between virtue and sin. Rather, it is a freedom beyond such choosing, a freedom based on and participating in God's very freedom.[28]

Divergences: God and Love versus Impersonal *Nirvana*

The greatest divergence between how union with God and existence in *Nirvana* are described is reflected in the character of union as love in John, as opposed to the radically impersonal experience of *Nirvana*. John describes union in a dynamic way. Since union—and indeed the entire path—involves knowing and loving God more directly and intimately, union is a relational reality. True, this is not a relationship like other relationships. When we say that we have a personal relationship with God we have to always remember that the term *person* is used here analogously. God is absolute mystery, and Being itself, not just another being one loves and relates to. However, union with God is indeed personal. It is a true, loving communion.

On one hand, the soul is totally and completely itself as it becomes empty of all possessions. And it lives focused only on the glory of God. This emptying of the soul corresponds to an emptying of the soul's propensity to objectify God or the self. Even in union, the intellect lives in a mystery. On the other hand, union is also an intimate knowledge of and sharing between divine lover and beloved, a possession of each other in love. John does not conceive of this mutual possession in monistic terms, as if the soul became fused with God and ceased to exist, but in the interrelational dynamism of lovers.[29] There is a paradox here, and both sides of the paradox need to be upheld. The soul is deified and lives as God, but the soul is also a real self, intimately loving and being loved. So while God cannot be objectified by the natural use of the faculties, and in this sense can never strictly be an object of love, God is never conceived of by John as anything else than a supernatural other, with whom one relates and from whom one enjoys deep, intimate, transforming love.

This loving union or this sharing of selves is not reflected in any way by the descriptions of *Nirvana*. Buddhaghosa describes the freedom of *Nirvana* as being free from any fear or desire. It is an existence where the powers of serenity and insight are in perfect balance. While it is indescribable, as is God for John, it is utterly impersonal. This is absolutely necessary. Buddhists, in this regard, wonder about theists speaking of a personal encounter with God. Theists describe God as uncaused, supernatural, and beyond all phenomenal reality. Buddhists use these terms to describe *Nirvana*. But because it is this, they object to any thought of having a *personal* relationship to *Nirvana*. Any kind of personal shared love or direct experience is, for them, philosophically impossible.

In addition to *Nirvana* being an impersonal reality, we also remember that Buddhaghosa's anthropology describes the self as ever changing and itself utterly impersonal. To suggest a real personal encounter is to sabotage the very philosophical foundation through which experience is interpreted. That *Nirvana* is impersonal is not experienced by Buddhists as a problem or a deficiency, but as the purity and fullness of truth.

Is *Nirvana* the same as God? Recall that many perennialists have argued that every religion has a name for its ultimate reference and that these names point to the same reality, whether described theistically, personally, impersonally, or in monistic terms. After all, when one is talking about that which cannot be objectively spoken of, that which transcends all things in the created word, and that which is described by virtually all as absolute mystery, in the end what is in a name? While this seems compelling at first glace, this comparative study suggests that such an easy identification is contrived. The most respectful conclusion that I can come to is that *Nirvana* and God are not the same realities described.

Unanswered Questions

A Life of Grace?

Instead of asking about the nature of God, absolute transcendence, or *Nirvana*, we could approach the question differently. At the end of the day, do both religions have essentially the same kind of liberation, even if they are conceived so differently? Here we see more promising possibilities. In many dramatic ways, the saint and the *arahat* do look dramatically alike in John's and Buddhaghosa's descriptions. They are both free of all detachments and free for loving service of others. The ego has died, and it is replaced in varying descriptions with a kind of self that is both empty and paradoxically completely actualized. Wisdom or *Dharma* works through the *arahat*. The Holy Spirit seems to work in the same way through the soul in union with God.

Some have argued that these spiritualities are drastically different. Buddhism is self-reliant, while Christianity is utterly reliant on grace. But really, in both, the initial life of the spiritual seeker is filled with hard work. The asceticism that both call for demands a great deal from the will. As one progresses in both paths, this dynamic changes. One could say that one receives more than one brings to the path. Christians definitively call this dynamic the life of grace, while Buddhists would reject such a category.[30] But do they correspond experientially? Several years ago, I interviewed four American meditation teachers who are among the most highly regarded teachers of Theravadin practices in the United States. I posed the question: In what sense can it be said that as we progress we *do* the practice less and it is more the case that the practice *does* us? What I was trying to get at was how closely progress along the Buddhist path was experienced like the Christian who is led by grace. The responses are as follows:

> STEVEN ARMSTRONG: The five factors of concentration can be so developed and integrated that we do not need to conger up these qualities. Instead, they arise naturally and engage experience without our trying. They do not need arousal, but we naturally stay with the flow of experience.

> CAROL WILSON: This means that there is a switch from "I" am putting out effort, "I" am putting forth the goal. Energy and the power of intention are not identified by the ego and one goes outside of the personality structure one is used to. It is giving up trying to lead the process from expectations or ideas and allowing this energy to happen as it happens.

> STEPHEN SMITH: The *dhamma [dharma]*[31] can overcome us and guide us. This is true in the sense that the *dhamma* is all within and inclined toward enlightenment. Ultimately everything becomes our practice. At first, we strive to connect right effort with concentration, and so on. As we progress, these energy levels more naturally converge to support the path. So we naturally are concentrated and see clearly. We seem to

work less hard at it. As the practice progresses we don't have to do much, since the energy is there. Mindfulness has the nature of seeing things as they are. We get anchored to the nature of seeing things as they are. We get anchored to this mindfulness. Practice is guided by these forces.

JOSEPH GOLDSTEIN: This is due to the growing realization of *anatta* and the *dhamma* [*dharma*] unfolding, and thus practice does itself. Mindfulness operates by itself and there is not much effort to it.[32]

From these descriptions, it seems that this sense of the *practice taking over* is not exactly what Christians would call the experience of grace. One might associate these descriptions to a skill one has, say woodworking, whereby one becomes so adept that one doesn't have to think about it anymore. It becomes part of who you are. On the other hand, it is possible that what these meditation teachers note is more aligned with the Christian experience of grace than we might think at first blush. Spiritual practice is not like other skills. Think of Smith's startling way of describing the dynamic of receptivity to the universal spiritual law: "The *dhamma* can overcome us and guide us." This is a language Christians use for grace. We could also consider what Carol Wilson describes as going outside of the self and letting the process guide one. Is this not the dynamic of passive nights of the senses and spirit? The issue could do for further analysis. In *Spirituality and Emptiness,* Donald Mitchell has suggested that some of the metaphors Christians have classically used to describe the experience of grace are strikingly similar to metaphors in many Buddhist circles.[33]

Is It the Same Saint?

Another approach to the question of whether both paths end in the same kind of liberation is to ask about what a saint looks like. Is the Christian saint, as John understands sanctity, the same kind of person as the Buddhist *arahat?* In some ways this is very much the case. Both are utterly free, completely open, perfectly ordered, and fully integrated human beings. Are they other-worldly? In some ways they are, insofar as they are not attached to the things or experiences of the world. In this sense, they have transcended the world even as they live in it. Both are absolutely aware of, but radically detached from, their own experience. And both enjoy perfect equanimity. It is because of this that, ironically, they are also the least otherworldly. For this very freedom also means that both are fully engaged in the world and in their experience. They aren't running greedily to pleasure or fearfully away from pain. There is a Buddhist saying: "A greedy mouth ruins the soup." That is, if our concentration is on gratifying the appetite, we actually do not attend well to our experience. We are ego absorbed. While if we are truly free from this greed, we find life all the more satisfying.

This is not only true of experiences but of relationships too. It is the person who is detached from one's ego who can truly love the other. When one no longer loves others simply as an extension of the self or to satisfy one's own needs, one becomes free to love them for their own sake alone.

The evidence that a Christian saint and a Buddhist *arahat* live in the same kind of reality is fairly compelling. I have had the honor of meeting and speaking to several great Buddhist masters, both from the United States and from Asia. If I hadn't known that they were Buddhists, but were told that they were Christians, I would have thought them probable saints. They radiated a quality of presence that was nothing less than spiritually profound. I recently asked the internationally regarded Hindu guru Sripad B. V. Sadhu Maharaja if holiness was really the same the world over. He replied, "Yes, I believe this. You can tell holy people immediately. They have a kind of vibration about them." As enigmatic as this seems, I believe that this speaks of a truth. There is a story of a Sufi mystic who dialogued with a Zen

Master. After their conversation the Islamic holy man said, "There is a Sufi inside you." And the reply from the Buddhist was, "I see a Zen Master within you."

On the other hand, we have already recognized that Christian and Buddhist notions of holiness are not easily aligned. Love dominates the Christian. I once asked Joseph Goldstein if love characterized an *arahat*. His reply was that it depended upon the *arahat*'s past *karma*. For some, this was true; they are very loving and warm. Others, however, were more distant and cool. Certainly compassion, this desire to assist others in their suffering, is universally understood as a Buddhist saintly quality. But love? This is not clearly the case. For John's version of the saint in union with God, love is the dominating theme from the beginning of the journey to its fulfillment. Love produces likeness, and to be like God is to love passionately like God. To be grasped by God's love—clearly experienced as such—is to fall in love as bride to groom. This marks the clearest, most dramatic difference.

Notes

1. Thomas Merton, *New Seeds of Contemplation* (New York: New Direction, 1961), 33; 60; 210; 283; 286–287 (with exclusive language adjusted).

2. See *The Catechism of the Catholic Church*, no. 1988; nos. 1996–1999.

3. Saint John of the Cross understands it to deepen throughout one's life. See *The Living Flame of Love* Pro.3.

4. See, for example, *The Spiritual Canticle* 26.10–11.

5. *Dark Night of the Soul* II.24.2.

6. *The Ascent of Mount Carmel* I.5.1. This dictum used in the beginning of *The Ascent* was intended to encourage the reader to withdraw all attachments to created things. But the dictum becomes applied throughout his writings to describe our becoming ever more like God as our souls become more devotedly attached only to God.

7. *Spiritual Canticle* 22.3; *Living Flame* 3.6; 3.24–25; 4.14.

8. *Living Flame* 2.33–34.

9. *Living Flame* 3.10.

10. *Living Flame* 3.6.

11. *Living Flame* 3.6.

12. *Living Flame* 2.34.

13. *Living Flame* 3.82. See also *Dark Night* II.4.1–2; II.9.1–5; II.13.11; II.21.11–12; *Living Flame* 1.3; 2.34; 3.78.

14. See *Ascent* II.26.3–8.

15. See Steven Collins's discussion on right views, *anatta*, and the relationship of *anatta* with *Nirvana*, in *Selfless Persons* (Cambridge: Cambridge University Press, 1982), 83ff.

16. See Walpola Rahula, *What the Buddha Taught* (New York: Grove Press, 1974), 13–15.

17. *The Path of Purification*, 16.67ff. This does not mean that his description of *Nirvana* denies the nihilist point of view regarding the self. That is a completely different discussion. Rather, he denies that *Nirvana* has no reference of its own except the annihilation of the self.

18. *Path*, 1.32. Technically, *Nirvana* is a reality, but not a phenomenal reality or a conditioned reality.

19. *Path*, 22.5; 21.18; 14.15; 21.24–37, respectively.

20. *Path*, 16.70; 22.5, respectively.

21. *Path*, 21.124; 22.127, respectively.

22. *Path*, 16.67.

23. For canonical descriptions of the literary use of *Nirvana*, see Rune Johansson, *The Psychology of Nirvana* (London: Allen & Unwin, 1969).

24. *Path*, 3.129.

25. *Path*, 1.5.

26. Edward Conze, *Buddhist Texts through the Ages* (San Francisco: Harper-Collins, 1964), 487–488.

27. *Living Flame* 2.34.

28. *Ascent* III.20.2–3.

29. See *Spiritual Canticle* 22; *Living Flame* 3.6; 3.24–25; 4.14. We see also that even in the utterly painful and spiritually dreadful purification of the dark night of the spirit there is an awareness on the soul's part of this divine other present within, purifying it in love. This is why when episodes of particularly painful experiences of purification diminish, the soul feels lost. While the soul is glad to be released from the pain of the purification, it also has lost the depth of its intimacy with Christ. See also *Dark Night* II.11.7.

30. That Buddhists reject the notion of grace is true for both Mahayana and Theravada Buddhists, but this is not the case with Pure Land Buddhism, which not only recognizes a kind of heavenly realm after death but also relies on the divine grace of Amita Buddha.

31. *Dhamma* is the Pali term for the more frequently known Sanskrit term *Dharma*. It means in this context the truth, way, or spiritual law of the universe.

32. Steven Armstrong, Carol Wilson, Stephen Smith, and Joseph Goldstein, interview by author, Barre, Massachusetts, December 15, 1994.

33. Donald Mitchell, *Spirituality and Emptiness: The Dynamics of Spiritual Life in Buddhism and Christianity* (New York: Paulist Press, 1991), 129ff.

Chapter Five

The Future of Dialogue: Interreligious Practice

What's Next?

In chapter 1, I raised the question of taking interreligious dialogue to another level, that is, the level of spiritual practice. In my opinion, this is the most exciting advancement for interreligious dialogue and perhaps the most critical one as well. I also believe that it is one of the trickiest parts of dialogue, and one given the least consideration in terms of method. In the field of spirituality, it is widely held that being actively engaged in the spiritual life one is writing about makes for the best scholarship. It doesn't replace hard study, nor ought one be presenting autobiography in the guise of scholarship. So one really has to exercise some critical, scholarly distance from the work. If this more objective distance can be achieved, however, actively practicing the spirituality one studies gives one an access into religious experiences and texts that outside observance cannot provide. If having an analogous experience to what one is studying is invaluable in the field of spirituality in general, it is all the more so in interreligious dialogue. One can listen to Buddhists or Hindus or Native Americans discuss their religious beliefs and practices, and this is crucial. But if one doesn't have some level of access into the real, lived dynamics of that faith, one is forever an outsider.

Recall that one of the great possibilities of dialogue is that it can expand one's horizon of awareness. We see things from another viewpoint and get an expanded sense of broader human spiritual experience. It may be that there are insights from another's tradition that actually complement limitations in one's own faith. Again, this is not license to become a spiritual dilettante. Before even entering into dialogue, one needs to be well grounded in one's own religious faith. Without this presumed, one becomes a weak dialogue partner. But dialogue opens up for us unknown possibilities. As mentioned in chapter 1, Thomas Merton suggested that spiritual practices of another religion could assist Catholic monastic renewal. Not only that, but I would argue that this is particularly the case with Theravada Buddhism, which understands its doctrine to be principally designed for spiritual practice.

Engagement into the spiritual practices of other religious traditions is actually now going on, even as theoretical considerations of it lag behind. I believe that this chapter can add an additional dimension to how interreligious practice can be considered, at least for the Christian. What are the possibilities? In what way, for example, could Buddhism add to the Christian experience of God or assist one's journey toward holiness? Are we seeking an amalgam? Is Buddhism an alternative practice that we can do alongside of our Christian piety? Can we remain loyal to our current faith and engage the piety of another faith? What is really being sought by such a venture? These questions we must address.

A Model for Interreligious Practice

In reviewing the literature I have discovered a number of prominent models for interreligious dialogue that currently serve as models for interreligious practice. They provide the next step from theory about dialogue to theory about interreligious practice.

Some are fraught with theoretical problems. Abhishiktananda (Henri Le Saux) and his protégé Bede Griffiths, for example, have taught that Christianity has to incorporate all other religious truths for it to be truly universal. Eastern and Western mysticism, they argue, complete and complement each other.[1] We could simply ask:

Is it true that for Christianity to be totally universal it must incorporate every profound spiritual way into itself? They particularly argue for integrating Hindu Vedanta into Christianity, since this solves the problem of Christian dualism.[2] If this is the case, then why stop at Vedanta? If we take this thesis seriously, then Christianity would have to incorporate Hindu, Buddhist, Jainist, Taoist, Jewish, Muslim, Native spiritualities, and so on.

Their position also begs the question of how one would be able to integrate all these spiritualities. This is especially problematic given that spiritualities are themselves organic and synthetic wholes. They each operate within a paradigm of philosophical, theological, and cultural considerations. And some of these spiritualities seem to conflict with each other. How can one simultaneously embrace the Hindu doctrine that *atman is Brahman* and the Buddhist insistence that there is no *atman*. We could also ask just how many paradigms one can actually integrate. Can one really integrate even two? I have found positions and inherent problems such as these typical in the literature.

In his most recent book, Paul Knitter persuasively argues for taking our postmodern context seriously. We first encountered the issue of postmodernity in chapter 1. Above all, the postmodern world is suspicious of theoretical models that try to subsume all paradigms of thinking or being into some glorious univocal plan. Knitter writes succinctly, "The religious traditions of the world are really different, and we have to *accept* those differences."[3]

Following Knitter's insight, and in light of the concerns I raised in chapter 1 regarding the perennialism so often presumed in comparative religion, I believe that the most helpful approach to interreligious practice is that of John S. Dunne. In three different works, Dunne has explored the notion of *passing over* into other ways of being and thinking. Fundamental to any growth, he argues, means that we have to *pass over* into a new experience or a new way of seeing things. This new experience is then integrated into what one already knows. The integration of such new insights or experiences is what he refers to as *coming back*.

In Dunne's first study, *The City of the Gods*, he explored passing over to other cultures to learn what other ways of living and understanding of life might teach us.[4] In *A Search for God in Time and Memory*, he was engaged in passing over to different lives, studying different standpoints from which human existence could be understood.[5] His final book in this series, *The Way of All the Earth*, investigated this passing over into other religions. In this final volume, he examined the nature of truth from the *Bhagavad Gita*, the denunciation of narcissism from the teachings of the Buddha, divine mediators from various Hindu cosmologies, spiritual integration in midlife from Muhammad, and knowing one's own spiritual essence from the Upanishads.[6]

A fundamental principle for Dunne is that nothing in human experience is fundamentally alien to others.[7] We all share a fundamental religious impulse and an inclination to truth. This core, shared human dynamic allows one to sympathetically enter into another's spiritual ethos. A second supposition for Dunne is that he believes that no one has the complete truth. This does not necessarily mean that Christianity is a relative religion along side of others. Rather, he would say that what is true about any given individual or group is also true of Christianity. That is, human beings and human ways of thinking are limited, even if they are informed and guided by revelation.

So *passing over* into another expression naturally broadens the mind and heart. And not only that, it is in passing over to another religious experience that one comes to see what is inside oneself that may have been dormant or poorly understood before the experience.[8] Dunne's *coming back* is what he calls the integration of that interreligious experience. Dunne never really addressed the issue of interreligious practice, but his approach can inform it.

Dunne's work is very akin to that of the comparative theology described by Francis Clooney. Clooney's method is to reflect on data from two (or possibly more) diverse religious traditions taken together. In so doing, new light might be shed upon the two sets of data, particularly that in one's home religion. Here reflection of the data of the other religion precedes any construction of theological judgments or conclusions. In short, comparative theology seeks to rethink and reunderstand the faith with which one begins.[9]

Dunne argues that one ought to simply allow the other to speak *as* other while suspending one's own sense of truth long enough to sympathetically enter the other's experience. Of course this entry is always quite partial and tentative, but Dunne shows that it really can be a valid passing. Dunne's work was not scholarly as such, and represented more of a project of spiritual reflection. However, it has had profound impact in interreligious dialogue. This passing over and coming back is the method prescribed widely.[10]

It is above all a tentative experiment. What one knows of the other's spirituality, even after investigating its texts, spiritual life, and spiritual practice, is not the same as living that spirituality throughout one's life.[11] Thus, such a procedure calls for a modesty of claims. Taking on another spiritual expression is forever an incomplete experience. No matter how nonconceptual *(apophatic)* a given meditative practice is, it necessarily involves another's philosophy of life; one that a Christian may not be able to share or integrate. One cannot extract a method of prayer or meditation as if it were utterly divorced from its religion's theology or agenda for liberation.[12]

The strength of Dunne's passing over method is that it allows others to speak for themselves. In this sense, it is classical dialogue methodology. The very experience of dialogue has the potential for deep transformation. We don't need to enter into it with a contrived assumption that the other has the same God, the same liberation, or even the same faith dynamic. We let the other speak *as* other. I also believe that the assumptions of this method are proper. Human growth is in fact a passing from what we know to what we have yet to learn. And it seems reasonable that human beings have great capacity for a sympathetic understanding of others, even those of another religious systems.

The possibility of suspending one's own approach to reality and truly experiencing another's life and religion also seems reasonable, especially if one's expectations are nuanced. However, it is only possible on certain levels. Can a Christian truly suspend his or her faith commitments and adore Krishna wholeheartedly and as Lord? This seems unlikely. To my mind, however, the modesty inherent in Dunne's approach is appropriate. While tentative, it is an approach that has real possibilities of gaining sound results. One can indeed get a true sense of the other. Of course, before one actually engages in another's religious practice, one does have to ask fundamental questions as to whether and in what ways such a practice is valid or responsible for integration into a Christian framework.

One of the problems in many models of interreligious dialogue is that they tend to overstate their theoretical premises. These presuppositions can control how dialogue or interreligious practice is considered or experienced. Dunne's method, on the other hand, presumes little more than that something good can come from entering into another's experience and creatively integrating the experience of the encounter. As we relate this method to the goals for dialogue, we can appreciate its inherent possibilities. It allows one to see oneself, one's own religion, and spiritual truth itself from another vantage point. We also come to a greater understanding of others' and their spiritual truths. This is the *crossing over*. In coming back, one's horizons are expanded and one may see striking elements in one's own tradition anew. Like all true encounters, it provides the forum for new truths to emerge. Because Dunne's method is nuanced and his theoretical presuppositions so reasonable, in my opinion his way is the best prescription for the way interreligious practice ought to be considered. It best represents the goals for interreligious dialogue, is actually the most open to the other *as* other, and is the least theologically problematic.

Possibilities for the Christian Use of Buddhist Practices

Limitations for the Christian

I believe, both theologically and from personal experience, that a Christian can engage in the spiritual practices other religious faiths. But I also believe that such a bold adventure has serious limitations, and these need to be respected. Specifically, I see three fundamental limitations: theoretical, theological, and practical.

The theoretical limitation comes principally from one of the great challenges of postmodernity and religious pluralism, that is, religions exist in paradigms. They provide ways of thinking about the world, oneself, transcendence, and so on. This suggests that one cannot fully embrace two religious paradigms simultaneously. Here the biblical dictum seems appropriate: "You cannot serve two masters" (Matt 6.24). Religious traditions exist as paths to an ultimate horizon. Even if the path is conceived as relative, one needs to wholeheartedly embrace it if there is to be any hope for real transformation. This gives the path a kind of exclusivity. Even if one believes that all paths lead to the same goal—itself problematic—one can only reach that goal with absolute focus.[13] Philosophically, we could say simply that you cannot violate the principle of noncontradiction. You can't hold two mutually exclusive beliefs at the same time. Regarding our study here, Saint John of the Cross and Buddhaghosa really do have radically divergent philosophies regarding the nature of human beings and that of absolute reality. You cannot hold them both together.

The theological limitation is simply this: The Christian has to come to the encounter with some form of Christic priority. To come to dialogue without this is simply not responsible to the faith one brings. If one believes that Jesus is Lord, and if this refers to something objectively true, then such a commitment influences how interreligious dialogue and practice is engaged. If Christ and loyalty to him is relegated to inconsequentiality, then the Christian has abandoned the very foundation for religious faith (and dialogue for that matter).[14]

For example, the Christian maintains the centrality of grace and love, and interprets advancement on the path by God's gratuitous love. One cultivates an attitude of dependence, humility, and gratitude. Such a concept does not really have a Theravadin analogue. A Christian ought to habitually cultivate an awareness of grace, cultivate a piety of reliance on grace, and recognize one's own inability to advance without it. In contrast, Theravada Buddhism insists in cultivating an attitude of self-reliance. In this sense, a Christian could never fully embrace a Buddhist path that undermines the very attitude of dependence at the heart of Christian piety.

The Christian path requires devotion to, submission to, and interpersonal experience of the trinitarian God. It seeks God's love as the central transforming agent. The Buddhist path denies as a false view that there is either a core lover or beloved, and its spiritual agenda takes this to the absolute degree. Of course, how a Christian understands such issues varies, but interreligious practice must be engaged in such a way that it corresponds to broad Christian spiritual goals and values.

Finally, there are practical limitations to interreligious practice. Even if one could find some kind of unification of religious truth, such that there would be no conflicts in embracing both paths, practically speaking the agenda is still limited. One rightly asks oneself: Can I really embrace two spiritualities? Does not my time, energy, community affiliation, necessary focus, and so on, limit the thoroughness with which I can embrace two (or more!) different religious traditions? Part of the method of Dunne's passing over is the acknowledgment that I can only have a limited understanding of the other. There are Buddhists who have heroically devoted their whole lives to seeking *Nirvana*, who have meditated intensely in Buddhist forms, in a Buddhist culture, and with a profound faith in Buddhist doctrine. To suggest that, as a Christian, I can pass over either completely or even substantially to a truly deep level of Buddhist insight and liberation trivializes the experience of those fully immersed in the Buddhist path.

Cooperating with the Christian Path

As is obvious, there are many serious limitations to interreligious practice. This does not imply, however, that extraordinary levels of rapprochement cannot occur. Interreligious practice could provide a forum for spiritual growth that a Christian may otherwise miss or fail to integrate to the same degree. We could ask: How would Theravada spirituality be incorporated responsibly by a Christian in John's contemplative tradition? How can it facilitate the Christian life of grace and union with God? I believe it can in many profound ways.

Conditionality and Impermanence

Buddhism understands all phenomenal reality as conditioned. Besides *Nirvana*, all else is relative. Buddhist philosophy teaches this and *vipassana* practice allows for it to be experienced directly. This insight corresponds to John's spirituality in profound ways. While for him the created universe has an inherent value, it is only valuable insofar as it is related to God as source and end of all meaning. John's spirituality also intends to break the aspirant from attributing any permanence or ultimacy to anything but the glory of God. The active night of the senses renounces all gratifications that are not aligned to God's glory and the active night of the spirit has a way of deconstructing notions both of oneself and God. Through the passive nights God draws the soul into a kind of total focus on eternal glory, making everything else quite relative.

The regular use of *vipassana* meditation would bring this insight into a kind of clarity that the proficient would not have before spiritual espousal. *Vipassana* meditation is a comprehensive meditative technique that demonstrates by direct experience the relativity both of one's experience and of all created things. It aligns profoundly with the active nights of the senses and the spirit, and it can contribute to the cultivation of these nights.

Impermanence is central to Buddhist insight practice. It is *anicca*, one of the three characteristics of all reality, that both terrorizes the aspirant and brings one to urgently seek *Nirvana* as that safe haven. The detachment process, which is the hallmark of John's active nights of both senses and spirit, could be dramatically facilitated by direct experience of the impermanence of our experience.[15]

In the first book of *Dark Night of the Soul*, John identifies seven capital *spiritualized* sins of a beginner. They can be reduced to the cultivation of pride, anger, and greed. Through *vipassana* practice, one comes to increasingly subtle levels of experiencing the impermanence of all reality. Here the inclinations of the unreformed soul are substantially reduced. One sees with great clarity the arising and falling of both virtuous (skillful) and villainous (unskillful and afflictive) thoughts. One sees one's own divisive thoughts with greater clarity, thus putting pride and the like in check. In doing so, one tends to deobjectify oneself in the process. These experiences highlight the unanswerable question: What is the subject of these prideful thoughts?

The experience of Buddhist impermanence functions in the same way to the other sins. With all things experienced as in flux, the soul realizes the absurdity of anger. Who's angry and at whom? With the ever-changing nature of people and events, the propensity to judgment is reduced in the same way. Finally, when one truly sees the impermanence of experience, one's greed is reduced. There's nothing like the Buddhist practice of meditating on a rotting corpse that works on one's greed and sensuality. Further, through *vipassana* practice one sees not only the ever-changing nature of desire, but also the illusory value of the object of desire in meeting any deep need. In sum, it is through Buddhist insight practices that one loses one's attachments to the very things that keep us from being free for God.

Crucifixion of Self

In Christian spiritual literature, one regularly comes across the terms *false self* and *true self.* I've addressed this periodically in earlier chapters. We die to our false selves and encounter our truest selves. Or in terms of vision, we break the illusion of the false self so that the truth of the true self is free to emerge. Christian spiritual transformation provides the possibility of experiencing oneself, the world, and God in an authentic, self-giving, spiritually enlightened way. John reflects this paschal language. The narcissism of the old man has to die so that the transformed, self-giving new creation may emerge. Christ's own crucifixion is the model.

Buddhist practice that facilitates realization of *anatta* (no-self) provides an excellent forum for this kind of dying to the self.[16] In *vipassana* practice, one's self-image is constantly confronted as an illusion. Wherever one would locate the self, through experience, conceptualizations, social roles, and so on, the practice of *vipassana* betrays this to be false.[17] The Christian paradox of the true self is that it is only true and free when it is disentangled from any form of self-objectification. Even, and especially, in union there is nothing to claim or cling to. That is, the sense of self stays ever deobjectified.

Buddhist insight into selflessness can be perfectly valid for Christian self-emptying as long as one retains the proviso that there is a great difference between John's detachment as it renounces objectifications of the self and Buddhaghosa's absolute deconstruction of the self. The deconstruction of the self in Buddhism, while sharing the agenda of breaking narcissism, also has the agenda of reducing the soul to an impersonal collection of aggregates. This latter agenda cannot be incorporated vigorously without undermining Christian spirituality.[18]

Detachment in Faith

There is one more element regarding the place that detachment plays in Buddhism and its appropriation for the Christian. This element involves faith. For John, recall that the active night of faith refers to the emptying of the intellect in meditation, as well as a general mindful repose and openness to the mystery of God in one's day-to-day life. Faith also inclines the soul to that which the soul cannot conceive through natural means, that is, God. Buddhist faith pushes the believer in the same way, but with even less direction. The Buddhist dynamic of faith also involves a kind of detached emptiness of any spiritual experience.

We recall that, in John, the long period of proficiency involves an ever more subtle awareness of God's love. Assuredly this stage includes many periods of dryness, and the soul should never try to assess one's direct spiritual experience. This is the great lesson in *The Ascent of Mount Carmel.* By and large, however, the soul can expect and prepare for recognizing God's presence (*noticia amorosa*—noticing love). Buddhist detachment insists on radical faith without any exceptions. It is not different from what John teaches except in emphasis: Expect absolutely nothing and trust the process.[19] This is sound Buddhist advice regarding the emptying quality of faith, and it directly aligns with John's.

Conclusion

We see here a striking correspondence in the way that insight practice *(vipassana)* is aligned with John's active nights of the senses and spirit. They do not correspond to the passive nights, since these are experienced as the transforming love of God. Rather, Theravadin practices provide different ways for the soul to accomplish the spiritual cultivation necessary to be present for transformation. This does not imply that Buddhist practices should be regarded as only human or natural, while the passive nights are supernatural. From a Christian point of view, any spiritual practice (be it Christian or non-Christian) directed to ultimate truth has God's grace as its foundation, its life force, and its truest end. And this would be true of the active nights as well. Any desire for truth and real spiritual freedom is, for a Christian, a response to and a cooperation with grace. In this vein, Buddhist meditation, particularly *vipassana*, ought to be regarded by the Christian on some level as truly spiritual. It is simply that we do not see the dynamics of the passive nights in the practice of *vipassana.*

Complementing the Christian Path

Back to Detachment

In the previous section we observed how Theravadin practices could cooperate with a Christian contemplative path. I also believe that these can complement or add to the Christian path as well. These practices can show us with new eyes what we would not otherwise see. It should be rather obvious by now that the central dynamic in the active nights is detachment. I described how the experience of Buddhist impermanence, no-self, and faith can facilitate this Christian detachment. There are two levels of detachment, which Buddhaghosa insists upon, that may well go beyond what is found in John. In insight practice *(vipassana)*, there are two principal strategies recommended by Buddhaghosa. The first involves an active deconstruction of the self by seeking and interpreting experience according to the three characteristics *(anicca, anatta,* and *dukkha).* The second is the *vipassana* practice of bare attention. One does not seek out these characteristics. Rather, one simply relinquishes all control. Whatever arises, arises; whatever subsides, subsides. One neither seeks anything nor expects anything. You do nothing more than watch these arisings and dissipations mindfully. This form of detachment, this radical cessation of any clinging, is very much a part of John's spirituality. I maintain, however, that the Buddhist practice brings such detachment to a new level. This form of piety cannot be central for the Christian, but it can augment the very spiritual dynamic that John teaches.

Passing World

The rigorous experience of impermanence and conditionality that we observed in Theravada Buddhism may assist the Christian in recognizing a Christian truth, but in even a more profound way: The world is relative. Saint Peter writes, "What we are waiting for, relying on his promises, is the new heavens and new earth" (2 Pet 3:13). In the same vein, Saint Paul writes about this world as an exile while "our true home is in heaven" (Phil 3:20). In Christian theology, the reign of God must always be grounded in the present world. Even regarding the eschatological reign, God's justice can never be divorced from this present reality. On the other hand, there is can be no utopia here. This is a passing world. Theravada practices bring this Christian conviction to clarity unparalleled in Christianity itself. We saw that, for both Buddhaghosa and John, detachment leads to skillful, non-attached love. I believe that detachment in Theravada Buddhism makes this actual nature of transience of the world even more obvious by experience. *Vipassana* practice shows how impermanence works in a way that the Christian otherwise would see less clearly.

Samadhi *Possibilities*

Thus far I have been exclusively focused on Buddhist insight practice *(vipassana)* in helping the Christian. I do believe that the Buddhist tradition of concentrative meditative techniques could also complement the Christian path. This would be less obvious, and in fact I believe, less helpful regarding such things as the *kasina* meditations. The divine-abidings meditations, on the other hand, provide something readily helpful. We observed in Buddhaghosa that the meditations on love, compassion, sympathetic joy, and equanimity balance and correct each other's weaknesses. Collectively, they give one a profound approach to our relationships. Buddhaghosa does not regard these exercises as curative, but they do balance practice and cultivate a pliant spirit.

One might think that such meditative techniques would be an impediment to the spirituality of Saint John of the Cross. We saw that the proficient ought to diminish and eventually eliminate all discursive meditation for the sake of this more direct, nonconceptual contemplation.[20] I would suggest, however, that these meditations would not act as impediments at all. The cultivation of intensive divine-abidings practice need not lead the soul to regress. Rather, it could have the same result for the Christian contemplative as for the Buddhist in cultivating a healthy, loving, detached mental state in which both contemplative prayer and right relationships may flourish.

The divine-abidings meditations are not used by the Buddhist as means of seeking absolute transcendence. Relative to *Nirvana* (and by extension, God), they are *mundane*. In terms of the mental cultivation they provide, however, they have been proven to be superb practices in bringing one to the kind of concentration that both Theravadin *vipassana* and Christian contemplation seek. In addition, taken collectively, they provide an engaged yet detached posture for one to be in the world.

Let us use the meditation for loving-kindness *(metta)* as an example. Typically, in Buddhist practice one begins this meditation by wishing goodness and blessings to someone very accessible to love. Usually, it is simply oneself. When *metta* arises and is solidly in place, the meditator extends this expression to another object of love to whom this would be easy, but for whom one has little emotional entanglement, such as a benefactor. The meditation follows this pattern of extension, moving to another less close to oneself, and so on, even to include another one has an aversion toward. When a high degree of loving-kindness arises and maintains itself in this way, the meditator then extends such *metta* to all beings, and eventually to every conceivable part of the universe. This overwhelming sense of loving-kindness then becomes the object of concentration, the whole mind being highly focused and awash with universal love and goodwill.

A Christian, even one following John's contemplative path, could easily embrace such a practice. One could also Christianize it. For example, one might take a Christian concept, such as the universal presence of Christ's love, and meditate on that truth using the divine-abidings meditational strategy. One could begin with the realization of Christ within. This is, in fact, the realization that has come to the proficient. One could also attend to one's natural feeling of joy or gratitude for this knowledge. One then extends that awareness beyond oneself to others for whom such a realization is easiest to visualize, such as a saint or spiritual friend. Following the formula, one could ultimately visualize and extend the meditation of universal divine love to the very atoms of the universe.

The meditation would be wholly Christian and sufficiently nondiscursive to keep one from John's warnings about the liabilities of mental or discursive prayer. Once sufficiently concentrated, in fact, there are essentially no thoughts. Because this is an act of meditative concentration, it would not properly be contemplative prayer. On the other hand, it would be a way to cultivate a Christian truth for the heart. And it would create, on a highly subtle level, a deep sense of universal love and gratitude. It would also conceivably create a greater sense of detachment, since the soul experiences this love of Christ as divinely gratuitous and as inclusive of all. There is no pride when the soul believes itself existing only by grace and existing in the same love as the rest of the universe. The soul sees that it drinks from the same gratuitous well as all other beings.

Critique of the Christian Path

In the previous sections we have been considering ways in which Theravada spirituality can conform to or complement what is a normative Christian path. There may be a further gift that Buddhism could bring to Christianity. It could highlight a deficiency that one might not otherwise recognize. One example is Buddhism's insistence on non-duality. This is not the non-duality of the Hindu Vedanta, which saw the *atman* to be identical to *Brahman*. Theravada non-duality refers to the interconnectedness of all things. We saw in Buddhaghosa's presentation this concept of dependent-origination. We have thus far looked at it from the perspective on the interconnectedness of the five aggregates and their formations. There is also dependent-origination on a macro level. In Buddhist philosophy there is no real separation between any sentient being. Everything is relative, everything is relational, and everything is interconnected. One sees this truth clearly in intensive practice.

One obvious example may suffice. One experiences on retreat that the mood of an individual meditator can affect the collective mood of the monastery or retreat center. This in turn affects one's personal experience in meditation, the very data of one's inner life. One is tempted to think that one's interior experience is one's own, having nothing objectively to do with anyone else's experience. What one finds out is that all inner experiences are somehow interrelated. On a larger scale, Buddhism teaches that all phenomenal beings interpenetrate each other's life, even physiologically.

There is no correlative in the spirituality of Saint John of the Cross. Buddhists, with their anthropology and impersonal aggregates, understand this as an ultimate truth. Such a truth, taken to the degree that Buddhists have appropriated it, would undermine the Christian conviction that people, while interrelated, are also separate and individual. So while Christianity could not completely embrace this macro level of dependent-origination, nonetheless, a heightened awareness of our interrelatedness that comes from crossing over and experiencing reality through Buddhist conceptions might provide a larger, communal dimension to John's more individualized spirituality.[21]

Notes

1. Bede Griffiths, *Vedanta and Christian Faith* (Clearlake, CA: The Dawn Horse Press, 1973), 73–74 and *Return to the Center* (Springfield, IL: Templegate, 1977), 60.

2. Abhishiktananda, *Saccidananda: A Christian Approach to Advaitic Experience* (Delhi: I.S.P.C.K., 1974), 11, 47–48, 68–69, 88, 104. See also Abhishiktananda, *Prayer* (Philadelphia: Westminster Press, 1972), 66, and "The Experience of God in Eastern Religions," *Cistercian Studies* 9, nos. 2–3 (1974): 152–153.

3. Paul Knitter, *Introducing Theologies of Religion* (Maryknoll, NY: Orbis, 2002), 173.

4. John S. Dunne, *The City of the Gods: A Study in Myth and Mortality* (New York: Macmillan, 1965).

5. John S. Dunne, *A Search for God in Time and Memory* (London: Collier-Macmillan, 1967).

6. John S. Dunne, *The Way of All the Earth: Experiments in Truth and Religion* (New York: Macmillan, 1972).

7. Dunne, *Way of All the Earth*, 230.

8. Dunne, *Way of All the Earth*, 180.

9. See Francis Clooney, "Sacrifice and Its Spiritualization in the Christian and Hindu Traditions: A Study of Comparative Theology," *Harvard Theological Review* 78, nos. 3–4 (1985); "Catholic Theology and the Study of Religion in South Asia: Widening the Context for Theological Reflection," *Theological Studies* 48, no. 4 (1987); and "Vedanta, Theology, and Modernity: Theology's New Conversation with World Religions," *Theological Studies* 51, no. 2 (1990).

10. See, for example, John Cobb's *Beyond Dialogue* (Philadelphia: Fortress Press, 1982). Cobb takes this model and asks what such a procedure would do for Christianity in relationship with Buddhism, especially on the level of shared practice.

11. Cobb, 98.

12. Cobb, 71.

13. Even Thomas Keating, who is an influential voice in integrating practice, points to this. At a certain point, belief systems simply clash. See Thomas Keating, "Meditative Technologies," *The Way Supplement* 78 (Fall 1993): 54–63. This is also the position of Winston King, who argues that every religious experience has an ideological context, no

matter how elastically that religion is portrayed. See Winston King, "Buddhist-Christian Dialogue," in *Religions in Dialogue: East and West Meet* (New York: University of America Press, 1985), 261ff. See also Cobb, 71.

14. For an interesting discussion on this point, see L. W. Barnard, "The Christian Approach to the East," *Theology* 61 (July 1958): 282.

15. John Cobb, "The Buddhist-Christian Dialogue since 1946: The Christian Side," in *Religious Issues and Interreligious Developments* since 1945 (New York: Greenwood Press, 1989), 282–283.

16. Basil Pennington, "Looking East—Seeing West," *America* 134, no. 9 (1976): 180.

17. See also Cobb, *Beyond Dialogue*, 72.

18. See Cobb, *Beyond Dialogue*, 81–86, and "Buddhist-Christian Dialogue," 582–583.

19. Cobb, *Beyond Dialogue*, 99–104.

20. Of course, this advice of John's cannot be taken literally. He himself prayed the Divine Office daily as well as went to mass daily. Both of these practices would follow under the rubric of mental prayer.

21. While radical interrelatedness has not correlative in John's spirituality, this does not suggest that it does not exist. In Mitchell's *Spirituality and Emptiness* (New York: Paulist Press, 1991), he describes the modern spirituality of Chiara Lubich and the Focolare movement. In Lubich's mysticism, interrelatedness through self-emptying love of neighbor is the very path to full participation in the divine mystery. Mitchell describes this not simply as a path of service, but rather as a vision of humanity in which our primordial nature is relational (see 158ff). We also see the impact of non-duality in Buddhist-Christian dialogue discussed by many others. See, for example, Paul Knitter, "Horizons on Christianity's New Dialogue with Buddhism," *Horizons* 8, no. 1 (1981): 46; Johnston, *Christian Zen* (New York: Harper & Row, 1971), 48; and Antony Fernando, *Buddhism and Christianity: Their Inner Affinity* (Colombo: Ecumenical Institute for Study and Dialogue, 1981), 103ff.

Epilogue

This small book has had a modest agenda. I have tried to provide one way in which to consider interreligious dialogue. Of course, the specific focus has been between a Theravada meditation and Christian contemplation. I have also tried to provide one way in which to consider a responsible Christian use of Buddhist practices. In doing so, I also hope to have articulated a method of consideration that can be extrapolated more broadly. So this book is not just about crossing over to Buddhism, but also about how to cross over to other religions as well. This comparative project focused on anthropology, the path, and the goal of that path. These are not the only comparative possibilities. One could include comparing, for example, the rituals in various traditions. Nonetheless, I believe that as a method it has wider possibilities. I believe that the analysis of interreligious practice is best made through the discipline of spirituality, since spirituality is best suited to analyze religious experience and the path that directs and interprets such experience. In sum, I believe that this is a solid method for addressing how religious experiences and paths interrelate.

But what are the limitations to such a method? And where should the conversation of interreligious dialogue progress? I would like to suggest two issues for further discussion. The most obvious limitation to this particular dialogue is that neither contemplative Christianity nor meditative Theravada Buddhism represent their respective traditions fully. I have argued that the spirituality of Saint John of the Cross is indeed representative of much broader and deeper Christian convictions of the contemplative path. But this is not all of Christian spirituality, and it cannot be said to articulate even all of monastic spirituality. For example, Benedictine spirituality has little or no appreciation for apophatic prayer as John describes it. Rather, *lectio divina*, that practice of always beginning prayer conceptually through the word of God and ruminating on the word through the day, remains central.

The same issue can be raised for Theravada Buddhism. While I have also argued for the centrality of Buddhaghosa's presentation, it is central only for those deeply involved in meditation. In fact, most Theravada Buddhists do not meditate at length. This is not to suggest that most Theravada Buddhists are poor practitioners of their faith. Rather, their religiosity is more ritualistically oriented. This is something that I have not dealt with here.

Thus, a limitation to this project is simply that what is discussed is not a comparison of two religions, but really of two spiritual expressions of two religions. Given this, one realizes that what one can say generally about an interreligious encounter, and how much one could extrapolate from it is not as great as one might be tempted to think. The question I pose, given the above consideration, is whether or not another method of pursuing interreligious dialogue and practice could be constructed to minimize such a limitation. Is there a way to further consider the issue of interreligious dialogue and practice in such a way that the participants could more fully represent their respective traditions? Or is such a limitation inherent to any meeting of traditions that are complex and polymorphic?

The second concern for the possibility of using this method has to do with the complexity of the project. This complexity can be addressed in two ways. First, it involves the types of spiritualities being compared. Second, it involves the possibilities of interreligious practice. In choosing the spiritualities of Saint John of the Cross and Bhadantacariya Buddhaghosa I chose something fairly easy to compare. But what if one were to compare spiritualities where, for example, there is no easily recognizable path? What if one of the spiritualities could not be conceived of in terms of a holistic paradigm? Would this fact sabotage the dialogue or the possibility of interreligious practice? Or would it actually make such a comparison easier?

Another consideration along these lines involves comparing spiritualities that will not compare conceptually. Again, in using Buddhaghosa's description of Buddhism, such a project was relatively easy. Theravadins take their doctrine seriously, and it is well articulated. But what about those spiritualities that are not so amenable to such correspondence? What about a dialogue that would be tantamount to comparing apples to oranges, so to speak? To maintain the metaphor, one could learn more about fruit by such a comparison, but not about the nature of apples. Nor would such an apples and oranges comparison help one to investigate the possibilities of cross-pollination. How would one adjudicate theological, spiritual, and praxis-oriented concerns in an encounter with a religious tradition that operated under completely different religious sensibilities, say between Christian and Native Shamanistic spiritualities?

The second way to address the issue of the complexity of dialogue involves the question of a Christian staying loyal to his or her faith. In using Buddhaghosa, again, I avoided more sticky problems. *Nirvana* is not another God; nor does one worship *Nirvana*. The Buddha was the supreme teacher, but he certainly isn't understood as a savior to adore. Thus a Christian in pursuing some parts of the Theravada agenda would not be disloyal to Christ. But what about other religions where it would be less easy to make such a claim? Even in Buddhism such an issue of loyalty could be stretched. In Pure Land Buddhism, for example, there is a sense of the divinity of the Buddha. Could one approach such a spirituality in one's crossing over without being disloyal to one's own Christian commitments?

I would not anticipate such a problem for the Christian with regard to the other two great Western religions of Judaism and Islam, since the God of these religions is the God of the Christian religion, variously conceived. Regarding the East, I also see little problem with Zen or Theravada Buddhism, or even with Taoism, which are nontheistic. It does become more problematic with Pure Land Buddhism where *Amita Buddha* is a *name above all other names.* Further, with regard to Hinduism, I see less a problem with such religious traditions such as Vedanta. But with Shiva worship, for example, whereby Shiva is known as God, such a problem becomes very serious. On the one hand, such a comparison with such a spirituality could provide great fruit for the Christian, since both spiritualities share so much in common. On the other hand, such a comparison, when it comes to interreligious practice, is far more complicated to consider.

A final concern involves the issue of evil. One example could be engagement with religions that are shamanistic. Within many shamanistic paths one must employ supernatural evil in order to negotiate oneself through the labyrinth of mystical visions. How would a Christian consider doing so that would not be spiritually disastrous for one's own faith? It seems to me that these issues yet to be addressed in the theological literature, nor are they specifically addressed in this study. Wrestling with them responsibly takes us to the next step of encounter.

Summary of Comparisons

John of the Cross	Buddhaghosa
Theological Anthropology	

Convergences

John of the Cross	Buddhaghosa
Unreformed soul constantly craves	Unreformed psyche constantly craves
Deluded ego as narcissistic center	Deluded consciousness believes in a permanent self
Will dominated by attachments	Will dominated by attachments
Remedy as asceticism	Remedy as asceticism

Divergences

John of the Cross	Buddhaghosa
Self is a real, substantial soul	Self as impermanent and lacking substance

Spiritual Paths to Holiness
Convergences

John of the Cross	Buddhaghosa
Asceticism as foundational	Asceticism as foundational
Detachment as freedom from suffering	Detachment as freedom from suffering
Detachment as availability to God	Detachment as availability to spiritual progress

John of the Cross   Buddhaghosa

Spiritual Paths to Holiness
Convergences cont'd

Deconstruction of self by nights of the spirit	Deconstruction of self by meditative insight

Divergences

Contemplation by God's initiative	Various forms of cultivated meditation
Practice of self-emptying love	Practice of analyzing phenomena

Final Bliss
Convergences

Soul lives in and through wisdom	Psyche lives in and through *Dharma*
Absolute freedom of the soul	Absolute freedom of the psyche
Perfect peace	Perfect peace

Divergences

Identification with God	No identification of self
Loving union with personal God	Impersonal entrance into *Nirvana*

Glossary of Terms

* Asterisked terms in definitions are listed as terms in this glossary

Active Night of the Senses

The active night of the senses refers to the soul's practice of detachment from sensual gratifications. It is the life of spiritual asceticism, and is commonly a prelude to spiritual development and the *passive night of the senses.

Active Night of the Spirit

The active night of the spirit is the soul's cultivation of perpetual recollection in God. Here the soul empties one's intellect regarding how God is to be conceived (night of faith); one's memory as to how God has graced one in the past and how the soul might anticipate God's grace in the future (night of hope); and one's desires or will as to how God might act on the soul (night of love). The active night of the spirit is a prelude and condition for the *passive night of the spirit.

Amita/Amida Buddhism

In Chinese and Japanese Buddhism, Amitabha (lit., "boundless light") is the Buddha who represents the state of pure consciousness. Amitabha Buddha is the center of worship in Pure Land schools of Chinese and Japanese Buddhism. He symbolizes mercy and wisdom.

Analogy of Being

While the Fourth Lateran Council determined that there is more dissimilarity between God and human beings than similarity, the analogy of being asserts that we can speak validly about God, even if by analogy, based on human experience. To identify God as love

123

or as good suggests that what we know of love or goodness as creatures corresponds in some way to God.

Anatta (Pali); *Anatman* (Sanskrit)

Anatta is one of the three marks of all phenomenal existence. It is Buddhist doctrine that there is no permanent, eternal, or independent self.

Anicca (Pali); *Anitya* (Sanskrit)

Anicca is one of the three marks of all phenomenal existence. It is Buddhist doctrine that everything (mental and physical) is impermanent, and therefore, nonessential.

Apophatic

Apophatic refers to an approach to God or an experience of God that does not correspond to human ways of knowing or acting. It is a form of spirituality that acknowledges God's absolute mystery, and is associated with *contemplation. In his *Life of Moses*, Gregory of Nyssa refers to this experience as *dark wisdom*, since it darkens the intellect to natural ways of knowing. Gregory describes it as a *cloud of unknowing*.

Araha(n)t (Pali); *Arhat* (Sanskrit)

An *arahat* is one who is fully enlightened, has extinguished all passions, has broken the cycle of rebirth, and has knowingly attained *Nirvana* in this life. An *arahat* represents the Buddhist saint.

Atman (Sanskrit); *Atta* (Pali)

Atman refers to the immortal soul in Hinduism. The *atman* is understood as beyond thought, body, or mundane consciousness. It is intricately related to, or sometimes absolutely identified with *Brahman* as an eternal and absolute being. The Buddha denied that there was an *atman*.

Beginner

In John's theology, a beginner is one who has been practicing a rigorous spiritual life of detachment and prayer. A beginner is one who is poised to experience or begins to experience the gift of infused contemplation.

Brahman
Brahman is the ultimate principle of transcendence in Hinduism.

Brahma-vihara (Sanskrit; Pali)
See **Divine-Abidings.**

Buddha
Literally, *Buddha* means "awakened one." The historical Buddha was born c. 563 BCE, a son of the prince of the Shakyas, a small kingdom in present-day Nepal. His first name was Siddhartha and his family name was Gautama (Pali: Siddhatta Gotama). Most Buddhists believe that Siddhartha was preceded by six other buddhas in prior eras, and will be followed by others. The historical Buddha is also known as *Shakamuni*, sage of the Shakya clan.

Buddhaghosa
Bhadantacariya Buddhaghosa was a fifth-century CE scholar who wrote numerous commentaries on Buddhist scriptures, and whose compilation of the Buddhist strategy to enlightenment, *The Path of Purification*, is one of the most widely read standard texts of the Theravada school.

Contemplation
Typically in Christianity, contemplation has been distinguished from meditation in that the former is nondiscursive, while the latter fully uses images or mental constructs in prayer. When the aspirant actively practices contemplation, this tends to be referred to as *acquired contemplation*. When the soul has been blessed with supernatural grace this has been termed *infused contemplation*. That is, God directly moves the soul without the normal use of the faculties of the intellect, memory, or will. See also **Signs of Contemplation.**

Dependent-Origination

Dependent-origination or *patticca-samuppada* (Pali) refers to the interconnected arising of all physical or mental formations. Each part of the person (**khandha*) depends on the arisings of every other part, all of which arise together and are mutually interdependent. In order to break the chain of rebirth (**samsara*), one has to recognize the relationships among desire, **karma*, and all phenomenal arisings.

Dharma (Sanskrit); *Dhamma* (Pali)

Dharma literally means "carrying" or "holding," and has various meanings. It usually refers to the cosmic law, particularly regarding the law of **karma*. It can refer to the teachings of the Buddha, and it can refer to manifestations of reality.

Divine-Abidings

Divine-abidings *(Brahma-vihara)* literally refer to divine states of dwelling. Collectively, they represent a level of Buddhist cosmology referring to a godlike state of rebirth. While these represent an extraordinary rebirth, like all rebirths they too are limited and subject to **samsaric* rebirth to another state when their lifetime ends. In terms of Buddhist meditation, these refer to important postures of concentration: (1) loving-kindness (**metta*), (2) compassion (**karuna*), (3) sympathetic joy (**mudita*), and (4) equanimity toward all beings (**upekkha*).

Divinization

Divinization describes the soul's full participation in the divine life by grace. While the soul or person does not become God by nature, it does become God by full participation in God's very life and activity through God's grace.

Dukkha (Pali); *Duhkha* (Sanskrit)

Dukkha is suffering or dissatisfaction and represents one of the three signs of all phenomenal reality. That life is *dukkha* is also the first of the **Four Noble Truths. Dukkha* also refers to everything in the universe that is conditioned by what is not ultimate, that is, everything that is not **Nirvana*.

Eightfold Path
The Eightfold Path represents the last of the *Four Noble Truths and constitutes the path to enlightenment. The Eightfold Path represents (1) right understanding, (2) right thought, (3) right speech, (4) right action, (5) right livelihood, (6) right effort, (7) right mindfulness, and (8) right concentration.

Four Noble Truths
The Four Noble Truths form the foundation of Buddhism. They are (1) All existence is characterized by suffering (dissatisfaction); (2) The cause of suffering is craving or desire; (3) Suffering can be brought to an end; and (4) The *Eightfold Path is the means for liberation.

Illuminative Way
Traditionally, the illuminative way describes the life of *infused grace and contemplation. It is the longest part of the spiritual journey for the contemplative, and is equivalent to being a *proficient.

Infused Grace
This term has been applied by the tradition to refer to grace given to the soul by direct or immediate means in an *apophatic manner.

Infused Knowledge
This term refers to the knowledge of the mystery and presence of God, given to the soul in contemplation in a direct or immediate means in an *apophatic manner.

Jhana (Pali); ***Dhyana*** (Sanskrit)
Jhana literally means "absorption" and refers to levels of meditative concentration. In Buddhist meditation there are four lower *jhanas (rupa-jhanas)*, which are characterized by a meditative form, and four meditational states that are without meditative content *(arupa-jhanas)*.

John of the Cross
Born in 1542, Saint John of the Cross is considered a preeminent
spokesperson for the interior life of contemplation to union with
God. John's greatest contribution to mystical theology is his
comprehensive and analytical account of the successive stages of
purgation, illumination, and union through which the soul passes
in its course toward union with God. He died in 1591.

Karma (Sanskrit); *Kamma* (Pali)
Karma is the universal law of cause and effect. Unless a deed is
intended by one who has entered **Nirvana*, it is produced by a
kind of volitional activity that creates *karma*. This volitional activity leaves traces in the psyche, which will ripen into an effect during one's lifetime or in a future life. For example, "good *karma*,"
created by the intention of generosity, will produce a positive
effect in the aspirant's life or future life. "Bad *karma*," created by
the intention of anger, will eventually have a detrimental effect.

Karuna (Sanskrit; Pali)
Karuna means "compassion" and refers to a posture of non-
attached care for all sentient beings based on a recognition of the
oneness of all living beings and the universality of suffering. It is
also a **Brahma-vihara* meditation directed toward cultivating a
universal care.

Kasina (Pali)
A *kasina* is a device used to attain meditative concentration. There
are ten in number: earth, water, fire, air, blue, yellow, red, white,
space, and consciousness. These ten form part of the traditional
forty objects of meditation.

Kataphatic
Kataphatic refers to an approach to God or an experience of God
that corresponds to human ways of knowing or acting. As a spiritual expression that is devotional or discursive with the active use
of the intellect in expressing one's faith or experience.

Khandha (Pali); *Skandha* (Sanskrit)

In Buddhist anthropology, the human being is made up of five aggregates or *khandhas:* materiality, feeling, perception, mental formations, and consciousness.

Mahayana Buddhism

Mahayana Buddhism arose in the first century CE. It literally means "great vehicle" and collectively represents one of the two great traditions of Buddhism. Mahayana is called the great vehicle because it teaches the possibility of liberation for a great number of people in various lifestyles. While Hinayana stresses the salvation of the individual believer, *Mahayana* stresses enlightenment for the welfare of all sentient beings. Mahayana itself is a collective term referring to various schools of Buddhism, including the Madhyamika and Yogachara schools in India, *Tibetan, *Zen (Chan), and *Pure Land Buddhism.

Metta (Pali); *Maitri* (Sanskrit)

Metta literally means "kindness" or "benevolence," and refers to a posture of non-attached love. Not only is *metta* a central Buddhist virtue, but it is also a central *Brahma-vihara* meditation directed toward cultivating a universal love for all living beings.

Moksha (Sanskrit)

Moksha refers to release or liberation from the cycle of rebirth. It refers to the soteriological goal of Hinduism as liberation of the soul from suffering and illusion. It marks the end of rebirths and is frequently identified as the soul's union with *Brahman.

Mudita (Sanskrit; Pali)

Mudita literally means "sympathetic joy" and refers to the happiness one has for the well-being of others. It is also one of the *Brahma-vihara* meditations directed toward cultivating a unitive sense of all beings.

Nirvana (Sanskrit); *Nibbana* (Pali)

The etymology of *Nirvana* means "to blow out," and it is often translated as "extinction." This is the goal of Buddhism. It refers to the *blowing out* of all **karma* formations and the breaking of the chain of the cycle of rebirths (**samsara*). *Nirvana* is usually described negatively as *unconditioned* or the cessation of suffering. It is the state of peace and freedom from attachments to illusions and self-centered desires.

Panna (Pali); *Prajna* (Sanskrit)

Panna literally means "wisdom." It is particularly understood as the intuitive wisdom by which one knows the nature of all reality as impermanent, self-less, and dissatisfying.

Pari-Nirvana (Sanskrit); *Pari-Nibbana* (Pali)

Pari-Nirvana or *final-Nirvana* refers to **Nirvana* after death. Most Theravadin Buddhists believe that *Pari-Nirvana* refers to total extinction of the self at death, while most Mahayana Buddhists believe that *Pari-Nirvana* refers to a state of existence that transcends existence after death in such a way that it holds no analogy with a conditioned life.

Passing Over/Coming Back

John S. Dunne's method of interreligious dialogue recommends suspending what we believe in order to sympathetically enter into the beliefs or experience of another religious way of life. This is the *passing over*. *Coming back* refers to a fully conscious return to one's earlier religious or theological sensibilities while striving to incorporate insights gained from the experience of passing over.

Passive Night of the Senses

The passive night of the senses refers to God's having dried up the soul's normal, **kataphatic*, or devotional prayer life so as to engage the soul in contemplative prayer. Here the soul's typical understanding or experience of God has been blocked so that the soul can incline to contemplative grace.

Passive Night of the Spirit

The passive night of the spirit is God's active emptying of the soul through the theological faculties of faith, hope, and love. John writes that the passive night "puts the sensory and spiritual appetites to sleep....It binds the imagination and impedes it from doing any good discursive work. It makes the memory cease, the intellect becomes dark and unable to understand anything, and hence it causes the will also to become arid and constrained, and all the faculties empty and useless" (N.II.16.1).

Perennialism

Perennialism is a collective term in the study of religions that postulates various interrelated convictions about the nature of religions, such as (1) All religions witness to the same ultimate reality; (2) All religions have the same psychic content; (3) All religions speak to the same underlying religious experience; or (4) All religions are paths to the same salvation.

Perfect

This is equivalent to the stage of union whereby the soul remains, at some level, always in union with God. It is the life of *spiritual marriage and *divinization.

Postmodernity

Postmodernity refers to an advance in intellectual culture beyond Enlightenment assumptions that truth can be ultimately synthesized. It holds that all human expressions of truth are culturally and historically specific, and thus, cannot assert an objective expression of truth.

Proficient

This is the stage whereby the soul regularly approaches and experiences God in a contemplative manner. Typically, this stage lasts through much of the contemplative's life. It is equivalent to the *illuminative way.

Pure Land Buddhism

Pure Land represents a school of Buddhism in China (Ching-tu-tsung) and Japan (Jodo-shu) founded in the early fifth century CE. The goal of Pure Land Buddhism is to be reborn in the pure land of a particular Buddha *(Amitabha)*. This school stresses the importance of faith in the power and active compassion and grace of Buddha Amitabha. The practice of Pure Land focuses on the recitation of Amitabha's name and in visualizing through meditation his paradise.

Purgative Way
Traditionally, the purgative way describes the beginning of the interior life. It is the life of asceticism, and corresponds to the way of the *beginner.

Religious Pluralism
Religious pluralism, in the context of Christian theology, approaches the theological enterprise in light of the presence of other religious traditions, taking into account religious claims beyond Christian revelation.

Sadhana (Sanskrit)
Sadhana refers to spiritual practice. For most Hindus and Buddhists, doctrine is primarily important insofar as it facilitates *sadhana*.

Samadhi (Sanskrit; Pali)
Samadhi refers to intense concentration of consciousness. In Buddhism *samadhi* is produced through meditations with an interest in tranquility *(samatha)* and mental absorption (**jhana*).

Samsara (Sanskrit)
Samsara literally means "journeying" or "wandering," and refers to the succession of rebirths that all beings go through within various modes of existence until the liberation of *Nirvana*.

Sankhara (Pali); *Samskara* (Sanskrit)
Sankhara refers to all volitional impulses or intentions that precede action. This is the activity of the will prior to enlightenment, and thus, it is an activity touched by narcissistic desire.

Signs of Contemplation

In two places John of the Cross provides three signs that the soul is being led into a contemplative posture with God. In *The Ascent of Mount Carmel* the signs are (1) One cannot make discursive meditation or receive satisfaction from it; (2) One lacks the desire to fix one's meditations on anything; and (3) One desires to stay in simple loving awareness of God without any particular considerations (A.II.13.2–4). In *Dark Night of the Soul* the signs are (1) One finds no satisfaction or consolation from God or any other creature; (2) One turns to God solicitously and with painful care; and (3) One finds an inability to use the imagination in prayer (N.I.1.2). The slight difference between these signs can be reconciled as to whether or not the soul initially intuits the subtle quality of contemplative graces.

Sila (Sanskrit; Pali)

Sila literally means "precepts," and refers to the basic moral obligations for all Buddhists. *Sila* is a foundation to Buddhism and a prelude to meditation.

Spiritual Espousal

Traditionally, spiritual espousal is a term that describes either bona fide *spiritual marriage or the last phase of the dark night of the spirit, whereby the soul becomes united to God in faith but has yet to experience full union.

Spiritual Marriage

Spiritual marriage is full union with God insofar as this can be achieved in this life. It is equivalent to being one of the *perfect, in the *unitive way. It is *divinization insofar as this can be achieved in this life.

Sutra (Sanskrit); *Sutta* (Pali)

Sutra literally means "thread," and refers to the teachings of the Buddha found in the Buddhist canon.

Tanha (Pali); *Trsna* (Sanskrit)

Tanha literally means "thirst," and refers to the constant craving of the unenlightened mind. According to Buddha's Second Noble Truth, the cause of all suffering is *tanha*.

Theological Anthropology

Theological anthropology is a central aspect in systematic or dogmatic theology that refers to the study of the human being as viewed through a theological lens. Issues about human nature, the relationship between body and soul, the relationship between creature and Creator, and so on, are questions directly related to a theological anthropology.

Theological Pluralism

Most commonly, theological pluralism describes the consciousness that within Christian theology there are a number of approaches, models, and methods to theology. Theological pluralism also asserts that these various approaches cannot be synthesized into a singular vision. A second usage relates to a Christian theological approach to other religions and the possibilities of salvation among those religions.

Theological Virtues

The Christian tradition has taken from Paul's letters (cf. 1 Cor 13:12; 1 Thess 1:3; Gal 5:5–6; and Col 1:4-5) three primary virtues of the spiritual life: faith, hope, and love. These are often directly associated to the life of grace, in contrast to the *natural* or *cardinal virtues* of prudence, temperance, fortitude, and justice. The tradition has associated three faculties of the soul with each theological virtue, even as they interrelate. Faith is associated with the intellect; hope is associated with the memory; and love is associated with the will.

Theology of Religions

Theology of religions is a subdiscipline in systematic theology that attempts to account theologically for other religions from a Christian point of view. Of particular importance in a theology of religions are two interrelated issues. First, a theology of religions considers how God's grace might be understood as active in a non-Christian religion. Second, a theology of religions attempts to assess if and how salvation might occur in other religions. Current popular models often distinguish between three positions. An *exclusivist* position holds no possibility of salvation outside of an explicit Christian confession. An *inclusivist* position holds that salvation is possible in other religions, although these would be implicit expressions of the grace of Christ's salvation. A *pluralist* position holds that other religions can be legitimate means of salvation without a reference to Christ's salvation. That is, they are legitimate paths in their own right.

Theravada Buddhism
Theravada literally means "the teaching of the elders." It is the only surviving school of the Hinayana ("little vehicle") school of Buddhism. Today it is widespread in the countries of Southeast Asia, such as Thailand, Burma, Sri Lanka, Laos, and so on. Theravada Buddhism developed between the death of the Buddha and the end of the first century BCE, and thus, Theravadins consider themselves the school closest to pristine Buddhism.

Tibetan Buddhism
Tibetan Buddhism is a form of *Mahayana Buddhism practiced in Tibet and neighboring Himalayan countries. The foundations of Tibetan Buddhism were laid in the eighth century CE. Subsequently, different schools of Tibetan Buddhism have arisen. The specific nature of Tibetan Buddhism is the fusion of early monastic rules and the cultic methodology of Vajrayana, and frequently Tibetan Buddhism is simply referred to as *Vajrayana* Buddhism.

Unitive Way
Traditionally, this term describes the actual life of perfect union with God in this life. It is equivalent to *spiritual marriage, *divinization, or the life of the *perfect.

Upekkha (Pali); *Upeksha* (Sanskrit)
Upekkha literally means "not taking notice," and refers to one of the most important Buddhist virtues of equanimity. It is independent of

all attachments and through it one cultivates an equilibrium that transcends all distinctions in others or experience. It is also one of the *Brahma-vihara* meditations directed toward cultivating non-attachment to experience or relationships.

Vedanta (Sanskrit)
Vedanta describes a Hindu philosophical and theological reflection on the Vedas, particularly the Upanishads, which attempted to provide unity to a more scattered witness in the classical texts. Of particular importance is the nature of *Brahman or absolute reality and the relation that *Brahman has to the created universe, particularly with regard to the self or soul (*atman).

Vipassana (Pali); Vipashyana (Sanskrit)
Vipassana literally means "insight," and it refers to clear recognition of the three marks of existence: impermanence, no-self, and suffering. *Vipassana* is also a method of meditation that is an analytical examination of all arisings and dissipations of phenomenal existence, particularly in one's personal experience.

Zen Buddhism
Zen Buddhism in Japan or Chan in China is a school of *Mahayana Buddhism that developed in China in the sixth and seventh centuries. The great Buddhist saint Bodhidharma is generally recognized as the key figure in bringing *Mahayana Buddhism from India to China. Zen is a religion of self-realization leading to complete awakening. The essential nature of Zen can be summarized in (1) transmission of the *Dharma by a teacher, (2) nondependence on sacred writings, (3) direct pointing to the heart, and (4) realization of one's own Buddha nature.

Select Bibliography

General Issues in Theology, Dialogue, and Pluralism

Abhishiktananda, Swami. *Prayer.* Philadelphia: Westminster Press, 1972.

———. *Saccidananda: A Christian Approach to Advaitic Experience.* Delhi: I.S.P.C.K., 1974.

Arai, Tosh, and Wesley Ariarajah, eds. *Spirituality in Interfaith Dialogue.* Maryknoll, NY: Orbis, 1989.

Bryant, Darrol, and Frank Flinn, eds. *Interreligious Dialogue: Voices from a New Frontier.* New York: Paragon House, 1989.

Byron, Michael. *The Poor When They See It Will Be Glad: An Ecclesiology of Symbol as Integral to a Socially Relevant Post Modern North American Church.* STD Diss. Ann Arbor, MI: UMI, 2000.

Carr, Anne. *A Search for Wisdom and Spirit: Thomas Merton's Theology of Self.* Notre Dame, IN: Notre Dame Press, 1988.

Clasper, Paul. *Eastern Paths and the Christian Way.* Maryknoll, NY: Orbis, 1980.

Clooney, Francis. *Theology after Vedanta: An Experiment in Comparative Theology.* Albany: State University of New York Press, 1993.

———. *Thinking Ritually: Rediscovering the Purva Mimanmsa of Jaimini.* Vienna: Gerold & Co., 1990.

Congregation of the Doctrine of the Faith. *Dominus Iesus: On the Unicity and Salvific Universality of Jesus Christ and the Church.* Origins 30 no. 14 (2000): 210–219.

Dawe, D., and J. Carmen, eds. *Christian Faith in a Religiously Plural World.* Maryknoll, NY: Orbis, 1978.

D'Costa, Gavin. *Theology and Religious Pluralism: The Challenge of Other Religions.* Oxford: Basil Blackwell, 1986.

Dhavamony, Mariasusai. *Phenomenology of Religion.* Rome: Gregorian University Press, 1973.

Dunne, John S. *The Way of All the Earth: Experiments in Truth and Religion.* New York: Macmillan, 1972.

Dupuis, Jacques. *Toward a Christian Theology of Religious Pluralism.* Maryknoll, NY: Orbis, 1997.

Gort, Jerald, et al. *On Sharing Religious Experience: Possibilities of Interfaith Mutuality.* Grand Rapids, MI: Eerdmans, 1992.

Griffiths, Bede. *Vedanta and Christian Faith.* Clearlake, CA: The Dawn Horse Press, 1973.

Haight, Roger. *Jesus Symbol of God.* Maryknoll, NY: Orbis, 1999.

Hein, Mark. *Is Christ the Only Way? Christian Faith in a Pluralistic Society.* Valley Forge, PA: Judson Press, 1985.

Hick, John. *The Interpretation of Religion.* London: Macmillan, 1989.

Hick, John, ed. *Problems of Religious Pluralism.* New York: Macmillan, 1985.

Hick, John, and Brian Hebblethwaite, eds. *Christianity and Other Religions: Selected Readings.* Philadelphia: Fortress Press, 1980.

Hick, John, and Paul Knitter, eds. *The Myth of Christian Uniqueness: Toward a Pluralistic Theology of Religions.* Maryknoll, NY: Orbis, 1987.

John Paul II. *Crossing the Threshold of Hope.* Trans. Jenny and Martha McPhee. New York: Alfred Knopf, 1994.

Katz, Steven. *Mysticism and Philosophical Analysis.* New York: Oxford University Press, 1978.

Knitter, Paul. *Introducing Theologies of Religion.* Maryknoll, NY: Orbis, 2002.

―――. *No Other Name? A Critical Survey of Christian Attitudes toward the World Religions.* Maryknoll, NY: Orbis, 1985.

Lakeland, Paul. *Postmodernity.* Minneapolis: Augsburg Fortress, 1997.

Lockhead, David. *The Dialogical Imperative: A Christian Reflection on Interfaith Encounter.* Maryknoll, NY: Orbis, 1988.

Merton, Thomas. *New Seeds of Contemplation.* New York: New Direction, 1961.

Panikkar, Raimundo. *The Intrareligious Dialogue.* New York: Paulist Press, 1978.

Race, Alan. *Christians and Religious Pluralism: Patterns in the Christian Theology of Religions.* Maryknoll, NY: Orbis, 1982.

Swearer, Donald. *A Theology of Dialogue.* Bangkok: Department of Christian Education and Literature, 1973.

Swindler, Leonard, ed. *Toward a Universal Theology of Religions.* Maryknoll, NY: Orbis, 1987.

Tillich, Paul. *Christianity and the Encounter of the World Religions.* New York: Columbia University Press, 1963.

Toynbee, Arnold. *Christianity among the Religions of the World.* New York: Scribners, 1957.

Buddhist-Christian Dialogue

Cobb, John Jr. *Beyond Dialogue: Toward a Mutual Transformation of Christianity and Buddhism.* Philadelphia: Fortress Press, 1982.

De Silva, Lynn. *The Problem of Self in Buddhism and Christianity.* Columbo: Ecumenical Institute for Study and Dialogue, 1984.

Dhavamony, Mariasusai, and Claude Geffre, eds. *Buddhism and Christianity.* New York: Crossroad, 1979.

Fernando, Antony. *Buddhism and Christianity: Their Inner Affinity.* Columbo: Ecumenical Institute for Study and Dialogue, 1984.

Ingram, Paul, and Frederick Streng, eds. *Buddhist Christian Dialogue: Mutual Renewal and Transformation.* Honolulu: University of Hawaii Press, 1986.

Merton, Thomas. *The Asian Journal.* New York: New Directions, 1973.

———. *Mystics and Zen Masters.* New York: Dell Publishing, 1967.

Mitchell, Donald. *Spirituality and Emptiness: The Dynamics of Spiritual life in Buddhism and Christianity.* New York: Paulist Press, 1991.

Nakamura, Hajime. *Buddhism in Comparative Light.* New Delhi: Islam and the Modern Age Society, 1975.

Pieris, Alosius. *Love Meets Wisdom: A Christian Experience of Buddhism.* Maryknoll, NY: Orbis, 1988.

Swindler, Leonard, and Seiichi Yagi. *A Bridge to Buddhist-Christian Dialogue.* New York: Paulist Press, 1990.

Walker, Susan, ed. *Speaking of Silence: Christians and Buddhists on the Contemplative Way.* New York: Paulist Press, 1987.

Wells, Harry Lee. *The Problem of the Phenomenal Self: A Study of the Buddhist Doctrine of Anatta with Specific Regard to Buddhist-Christian Dialogue.* PhD Diss. Ann Arbor, MI: UMI, 1988.

Saint John of the Cross

Primary Texts

John of the Cross, Saint. *The Collected Works of St. John of the Cross* (rev.). Trans. and ed. Kavanaugh and Rodriquez. Washington, DC: ICS, 1991.

San Juan de la Cruz. *Obras Completas* [2 vols.]. Edicion de Luce Lopez-Baralt y Eulogio Pacho. Madrid: Alianza Editorial, 1991.

Secondary Texts

Brenan, Gerald. *St. John of the Cross: His Life and Poetry.* London: Cambridge University Press, 1973.

Burrows, Ruth. *Ascent to Love: The Spiritual Teaching of St. John of the Cross.* London: Darton, Longman and Todd, 1987.

Crisógono, de Jesús. *The Life of St. John of the Cross.* Trans. Kathleen Pond. London: Longmans, 1958.

Cugno, Alain. *St. John of the Cross: Reflections on Mystical Experiences.* Trans. Barbara Wall. New York: Seabury Press, 1982.

Edwards, James Denis. *The Dynamism in Faith: The Interaction between Experience of God and Explicit Faith: A Comparative Study of the Mystical Theology of John of the Cross and the Transcendental Theology of Karl Rahner.* PhD Diss. Ann Arbor, MI: UMI, 1979.

Gaudreau, Marie. *Mysticism and Image in St. John of the Cross.* Bern: Herbert Lang, 1976.

Hardy, Richard. *Search for Nothing: The Life of St. John of the Cross.* New York: Crossroad, 1982.

Hovley, Vincent. *Love in St. John of the Cross: A Contribution to Spiritual Theology.* PhD Diss. Ann Arbor, MI: UMI, 1978.

Kane, Thomas. *Gentleness in John of the Cross.* Oxford: SLG Press, 1985.

Maio, Eugene. *St. John of the Cross: The Imagery of Eros.* Madrid: Collecion Plaza Mayor Scholar, 1973.

McMahon, John. *The Divine Union in the Subida Del Monte Carmelo and the Nocha Oscura of St. John of the Cross.* PhD Diss. Washington, DC: Catholic University of America Press, 1941.

O'Donoghue, Noel. *Mystics for Our Time: Carmelite Meditations for a New Age.* Edinburgh: T & T Clark, 1989.

Payne, Steven, ed. *Carmelite Studies, VI.* Washington, DC: ICS, 1992.

Payne, Steven. *St. John of the Cross and the Cognitive Value of Mysticism: An Analysis of Sanjuanist Teaching and Its Philosophical Implications for Contemporary Discussions of Mystical Experience.* Boston: Kluwer Academic Publishers, 1990.

Ruiz, Frederico, et al. *God Speaks in the Night: The Life, Times, and Teachings of St. John of the Cross.* Trans. K. Kavavaugh. Washington, DC: ICS Publications, 1991.

Steggint, Otger, ed. *Juan de la Cruz: Espíritu de Llama.* Kampen, The Netherlands: Kok Pharos Publishing House, 1991.

Thompson, Colin. *The Poet and Mystic: A Study of the Cantico Espiritual of San Juan de la Cruz.* New York: Oxford University Press, 1977.

Toft, Evelyn. *San Juan de la Cruz: A New Perspective on Contemplation.* PhD Diss., University of Cincinnati, 1983.

Welch, John. *When Gods Die: An Introduction to St. John of the Cross.* New York: Paulist Press, 1990.

Wilhelmsen, Elizabeth. *Cognition and Communication in John of the Cross.* New York: P. Lang, 1985.

Theravada Buddhism

Primary Texts

Buddhaghosa, Bhadantacariya. *Visuddhimagga.* Rev. Dharmananda Kosambi and ed. Henri Clark Warren. Delhi: Motilal Banarsadass, 1950.

———. *The Path of Purification (Visuddhimagga).* Trans. Nanamoli. Kandy: Buddhist Publication Society, 1991.

Secondary Texts

Adikarem, E. W. *The Early History of Buddhism in Ceylon.* Dehiwala, Sri Lanka: Buddhist Cultural Centre, 1946.

Bond, George. "The Arahant: *Sainthood in Theravada Buddhism.*" In *Sainthood: Its Manifestations in World Religions.* Kieckhefer and Bond, eds. Berkeley: University of California Press, 1988, pp. 140–171.

Buswell, Robert E. Jr., and Robert M. Gimello, eds. *Paths to Liberation: The Marga and Its Transformations in Buddhist Thought.* Honolulu: University of Hawaii Press, 1992.

Collins, Steven. *Selfless Persons: Imagery and Thought in Theravada Buddhism.* Cambridge: Cambridge University Press, 1982.

Conze, Edward. *Buddhist Texts through the Ages.* San Francisco: Harper-Collins, 1964.

Dumoulin, Heinrich, ed. *Buddhism in the Modern World.* New York: Macmillan Publishing, 1976.

Goldstein, Joseph. *The Experience of Insight: A Simple and Direct Guide to Buddhist Meditation.* Boston: Shambhala, 1987.

———. *Transforming the Mind, Healing the World.* New York: Paulist Press, 1994.

Goldstein, Joseph, and Jack Kornfield. *Seeking the Heart of Wisdom: The Path of Insight Meditation.* Boston: Shambhala, 1987.

Griffiths, Paul. *On Being Mindless: Buddhist Meditation and the Mind-Body Problem.* La Salle, IL: Open Court, 1986.

Gunarantana, Henepola. *Mindfulness in Plain English.* Boston: Wisdom Publications, 1991.

———. *The Path of Serenity and Insight: An Explanation of Buddhist Jhanas.* Delhi: Motilal Benarsidass, 1985.

Johansson, Rune. *The Psychology of Nirvana.* London: Allen & Unwin, 1969.

Kalupahana, David. *Buddhist Philosophy: An Historical Analysis.* Honolulu: University Press of Hawaii, 1976.

———. *The Principles of Buddhist Psychology.* Albany: State University of New York Press, 1987.

Khantipalo, Bhikkhu. *Calm and Insight: A Buddhist Manual for Meditators.* London: Curxon Press, 1981.

King, Winston. *Theravada Meditation: The Buddhist Transformation of Yoga*. University Park: Pennsylvania State University Press, 1980.

Law, Bimala Charan. *The Life and Work of Buddhaghosa*. Delhi: Nag Publishers, 1976.

Lester, Robert. *Theravada Buddhism in Southeast Asia*. Ann Arbor: University of Michigan Press, 1973.

Nyanaponika, Thera. *The Heart of Buddhist Meditation*. York Beach, ME: Samuel Weiser, Inc., 1965.

———. *The Vision of Dhamma*. London: Rider, 1986.

Nyanatiloka, Thera. *Path to Deliverance*. Colombo: Bauddha Sahitya Sahbha, 1952.

Rahula, Walpola. *What the Buddha Taught* (rev.). New York: Grove Press, 1974.

Sayadaw, Mahasi. *The Progress of Insight through the Stages of Purification*. Trans. Nyanaponika Thera. Kandy: Forest Hermitage Press, 1965.

———. *The Satipatthana Vipassana Meditation*. Trans. U Pe Thin. San Francisco: Unity Press, 1971.

Silananda, U. *The Four Foundations of Mindfulness*. Boston: Wisdom Publications, 1990.

Soma, Thera. *The Way of Mindfulness: The Satipattana Sutta and Commentary*. Kandy: Buddhist Publication Society, 1975.

U Pandita, Sayadaw. *In This Very Life: The Liberation Teachings of the Buddha*. Trans. U Aggacitta. Boston: Wisdom Publications, 1991.

Vajiranana, Pravahera. *Buddhist Meditation in Theory and Practice*. Kuala Lumpur, Malaysia: Buddhist Missionary Society, 1962.

Wells, Harry Lee. *The Problem with the Phenomenal Self: A Study of the Buddhist Doctrine of Anatta with Specific Regard to Buddhist-Christian Dialogue*. PhD Diss. Southern Baptist Theological Seminary, 1988.

Yoshinori, Takeuchi. *The Heart of Buddhism: In Search of the Timeless Spirit of Primitive Buddhism*. Trans. and ed. James Heisig. New York: Crossroad, 1983.

Suggested Readings

General Issues in Theology, Dialogue, and Pluralism

Abhishiktananda, Swami [Henri Le Saux]. "The Experience of God in Eastern Religions." *Cistercian Studies* 9 nos. 2–3 (1974): 148–157.

———. *Prayer.* Philadelphia: Westminster Press, 1972.

———. *Saccidananda: A Christian Approach to Advaitic Experience.* Delhi: I.S.P.C.K., 1974.

Amaladoss, Michael. "Rationales for Dialogue with World Religions." *Origins* 19 no. 35 (1990): 572–577.

———. "The Spirituality of Dialogue." *Studies in Interreligious Dialogue* 3 no. 1 (1993): 58–70.

Arai, Tosh, and Wesley Ariarajah, eds. *Spirituality in Interfaith Dialogue.* Maryknoll, NY: Orbis, 1989.

Badham, Paul. "John Hick and the Human Response to Transcendent Reality." *Dialogue and Alliance* 5 no. 2 (1991): 43–51.

Barnes, Michael. "Beyond Inclusivism." *Heythrop* 30 no. 3 (1989): 325–327.

———. "On Not Including Everything: Christ, the Spirit, and the Other." *The Way Supplement* 78 (Fall 1993): 3–12.

Borelli, John. "Reflections on Letter to the Bishops of the Catholic Church on Some Aspects of Christian Meditation." *Buddhist-Christian Studies* 11 (1991): 139–147.

Bryant, Darrol, and Frank Flinn, eds. *Interreligious Dialogue: Voices from a New Frontier.* New York: Paragon House, 1989.

Burgess, Joseph. "Purpose, Problems, and Possibilities of Interreligious Dialogue." *Drew Gateway* 58 no. 3 (1989): 16–21.

Byron, Michael. *The Poor When They See It Will Be Glad: An Ecclesiology of Symbol as Integral to a Socially Relevant Post Modern North American Church.* STD Diss. Ann Arbor, MI: UMI, 2000.

Carr, Anne. *A Search for Wisdom and Spirit: Thomas Merton's Theology of Self.* Notre Dame, IN: Notre Dame Press, 1988.

Clasper, Paul. *Eastern Paths and the Christian Way.* Maryknoll, NY: Orbis, 1980.

Clooney, Francis. "Catholic Theology and the Study of Religion in South Asia: Widening the Context for Theological Reflection." *Theological Studies* 48 no. 4 (1987).

———. "Christianity and World Religions: Religion, Reason, and Pluralism." *Religious Studies Review* 15 no. 3 (1989): 197–203.

———. "Sacrifice and Its Spiritualization in the Christian and Hindu Traditions: A Study in Comparative Theology." *Harvard Theological Review* 78 nos. 3–4 (1985): 361–380.

———. *Theology after Vedanta: An Experiment in Comparative Theology.* Albany: State University of New York Press, 1993.

———. *Thinking Ritually: Rediscovering the Purva Mimanmsa of Jaimini.* Vienna: Gerold & Co., 1990.

———. "Vedanta, Theology, and Modernity: Theology's New Conversation with World Religions." *Theological Studies* 51 no. 2 (1990): 268–285.

Congregation of the Doctrine of the Faith. *Dominus Iesus: On the Unicity and Salvific Universality of Jesus Christ and the Church.* Origins 30 no. 14 (2000): 210–219.

Cousins, Ewert. "The Nature of Faith in Interreligious Dialogue." *The Way Supplement* 78 (Fall 1993): 32–41.

Coward, Howard. "Panikkar's Approach to Interreligous Dialogue." *Cross Currents* 29 no. 2 (1979): 183–189.

Dawe, D., and J. Carmen, eds. *Christian Faith in a Religiously Plural World.* Maryknoll, NY: Orbis, 1978.

D'Costa, Gavin. "Karl Rahner's Anonymous Christianity: A Reappraisal." *Modern Theology* 1 no. 2 (1985): 131–148.

———. *Theology and Religious Pluralism: The Challenge of Other Religions.* Oxford: Basil Blackwell, 1986.

Dhavamony, Mariasusai. *Phenomenology of Religion.* Rome: Gregorian University Press, 1973.

Doore, G. L. "Religion within the Limits of the Quest for the Highest Good." *Religious Studies* 19 no. 3 (1983): 345–359.

Dunne, John S. *The City of the Gods: A Study in Myth and Mortality.* New York: Macmillan, 1965.

———. *A Search for God in Time and Memory.* London: Collier-Macmillan, 1967.

———. *The Way of All the Earth: Experiments in Truth and Religion.* New York: Macmillan, 1972.

Dupuis, Jacques. *Toward a Christian Theology of Religious Pluralism.* Maryknoll, NY: Orbis, 1997.

Eck, Diana. "In the Name of Religions." *Wilson Quarterly* 17 no. 4 (1993): 90–100.

———. "On Seeking and Finding the World's Religions." *Christian Century* 107 no. 15 (1990): 454–456.

Eliade, Mircea. *Patterns in Comparative Religion.* Trans. Rosemary Sheed. New York: Sheed & Ward, 1958.

Eliade, Mircea, and Joseph Kitagawa, eds. *The History of Religions: Essays and Methodology.* Chicago: University of Chicago Press, 1959.

Fernando, Antony. "The Asian Oblate Seminar: Guidelines for Christians Engaged in Dialogue with Buddhists." *Lumen Vitae* 30 no. 1 (1975): 125–128.

Frick, Eugene. "The World Religions: Four Dimensions of a Catholic Hermeneutic." *Journal of Ecumenical Studies* 11 no. 4 (1974): 661–675.

Give, Bernard de. *"Á la recontre des moines hindouists et bouddhists Inde."* *Communicates et ligurgies* 61 no. 5 (1979): 461–469.

Gort, Jerald, et al. *On Sharing Religious Experience: Possibilities of Interfaith Mutuality.* Grand Rapids, MI: Eerdmans, 1992.

Grant, Colin. "The Threat and Prospect in Religious Pluralism." *Ecumenical Review* 41 no. 1 (1989): 50–63.

Griffiths, Bede. *Return to the Centre.* London: Collins, 1976.

———. *Vedanta and Christian Faith.* Clearlake, CA: The Dawn Horse Press, 1973.

Haight, Roger. *Jesus Symbol of God.* Maryknoll, NY: Orbis, 1999.

Hall, Thor. "Paul Knitter's Presuppositions for Interfaith Dialogue: A Critique." *Perspectives in Religious Studies* 17 (1990): 43–52.

Hein, Mark. *Is Christ the Only Way? Christian Faith in a Pluralistic Society.* Valley Forge, PA: Judson Press, 1985.

Hick, John. *The Interpretation of Religion.* London: Macmillan, 1989.

———, ed. *The Myth of God Incarnate.* London: SCM Press, 1977.

———, ed. *Problems of Religious Pluralism.* London: Macmillan, 1985.

Hick, John, and Brian Hebblethwaite, eds. *Christianity and Other Religions: Selected Readings.* Philadelphia: Fortress Press, 1980.

Hick, John, and Paul Knitter, eds. *The Myth of Christian Uniqueness: Toward a Pluralistic Theology of Religions.* Maryknoll, NY: Orbis, 1987.

Hocking, Ernest. *Living Religions in a World of Faith.* London: Allen & Unwin, 1940.

———. *Re-Thinking Missions.* New York: Harper & Row, 1932.

Hoeler, Harry. "Dialogue: Towards a Definition." *Unitarian Universalist Christian* 45 nos. 2–4 (1990): 112–126.

Hwang, Philip. "Interreligious Dialogue: Its Reasons, Attitudes, and Necessary Assumptions." *Dialogue and Alliance* 3 no. 1 (1989): 5–15.

Ingram, Paul. "Two Western Models of Interreligious Dialogue." *Journal of Ecumenical Studies* 26 no. 1 (1989): 8–28.

Jadot, Archbishop Jean. "The Church and the World's Religions: The Dialogue of Life." *Origins* 12 no. 46 (1983): 745–753.

James, William. *Varieties of Religious Experience.* New York: American Library of World Literature, 1958.

John Paul II. *Crossing the Threshold of Hope.* Trans. Jenny and Martha McPhee. New York: Alfred Knopf, 1994.

———. "John Paul II in India: Address to Non-Christian Leaders." *Origins* 15 no. 36 (1986): 597–598.

———. "The Meaning of the Assisi Day of Prayer." *Origins* 16 no. 31 (1987): 561–563.

———. *"Redemptor Hominis."* *Origins* 8 no. 40 (1979): 625–644.

———. *"Redemptoris Missio."* *Origins* 20 no. 34 (1991): 541–568.

Katz, Steven. *Mysticism and Philosophical Analysis.* New York: Oxford University Press, 1978.

Keating, Thomas. "Meditative Technologies." *The Way Supplement* 78 (Fall 1993): 54–63.

Knitter, Paul. "Horizons on Christianity's New Dialogue with Buddhism." *Horizons* 8 no. 1 (1981).

———. *Introducing Theologies of Religion.* Maryknoll, NY: Orbis, 2002.

———. "Key Questions for a Theology of Religions." *Horizons* 17 no. 1 (1990): 92–102.

———. *No Other Name? A Critical Survey of Christian Attitudes toward the World Religions.* Maryknoll, NY: Orbis, 1985.

———. "The Pluralist Move and Its Critics." *Drew Gateway* 58 no. 1 (1989): 1–16.

Kramer, Kenneth. "A Silent Dialogue: The Intrareligious Dimension." *Buddhist-Christian Studies* 10 (1990): 127–132.

Lakeland, Paul. *Postmodernity.* Minneapolis: Augsburg Fortress, 1997.

Lipner, Julius. "The 'Inter' of Interfaith Spirituality." *The Way Supplement* 78 (Fall 1993): 64–70.

Lockhead, David. *The Dialogical Imperative: A Christian Reflection on Interfaith Encounter.* Maryknoll, NY: Orbis, 1988.

Luck, Donald. "Christian Responses to Other Religions. Part II: A Bibliographical Overview." *Trinity Seminary Review* 12 no. 1 (1990): 3–13.

Masutani, Fumio. *A Comparative Study of Buddhism and Christianity.* Tokyo: Ciib Press, 1957.

Mejia, Jorge. "World Religions: Together to Pray." *Origins* 16 no. 21 (1986): 367–369.

Merton, Thomas. *New Seeds of Contemplation.* New York: New Direction, 1961.

Minnema, Lourens. "A Common Ground for Comparing Mystical Thought: Nishitani and Rahner from an Anthropological Perspective." *Japanese Religions* 17 no. 1 (1992): 50–74.

Mitchell, Donald. "A Revealing Dialogue." *The Way Supplement* 78 (Fall 1993): 42–53.

Moffit, John. "The Bhagavad Gita as Way-Shower to the Transcendental." *Theological Studies* 38 no. 2 (1977): 316–331.

Nygren, Anders. *Meaning and Method: Prolegomena to a Scientific Philosophy of Religion and a Scientific Theology.* Philadelphia: Fortress Press, 1972.

Otto, Rudolf. *The Idea of the Holy.* New York: Oxford University Press, 1958.

Panikkar, Raimundo. "The Bostonian Verities: A Comment on the Boston Affirmations." *Andover Newton Quarterly* 18 no. 3 (1978): 145–153.

———. "The Category of Growth in Comparative Religion: A Critical Self-Examination." *Harvard Theological Review* 66 no. 1 (1973): 113–140.

———. "The Crux of Christian Ecumenism: Can Universality and Chosenness be Held Simultaneously?" *Journal of Ecumenical Studies* 26 no. 1 (1989): 82–99.

———. "Faith and Belief: A Multireligious Experience." *Anglican Theological Review* 53 no. 4 (1971): 219–237.

———. *The Intrareligious Dialogue.* New York: Paulist Press, 1978.

———. "The Myth of Pluralism: The Tower of Babel—a Dedication on Non-violence." *Cross Currents* 29 no. 2 (1979): 197–220.

Parekh, Bhikhu. "The Concept of Inter-Faith Dialogue." *Faith and Freedom* 42 no. 1 (1989): 4–12.

Paul VI. *Ecclesiam Suam* (Encyclical letter on the Mission of the Church). Glen Rock, NJ: Paulist Press, 1964.

Pontifical Council for Interreligious Dialogue. "The Attitude of the Church towards the Followers of Other Religions." *Bulletin* 19 no. 2 (1984): 126–141.

Race, Alan. "Christianity and Other Religions: Is Inclusivism Enough?" *Theology* 89 (May 1986): 178–186.

———. *Christians and Religious Pluralism: Patterns in the Christian Theology of Religions.* Maryknoll, NY: Orbis, 1982.

Rahner, Karl. *Theological Investigations,* Vol. 3. Trans. Karl Kruger. Baltimore: Halcion Press, 1966.

———. *Theological Investigations,* Vol. 6. Trans. Karl Kruger. Baltimore: Halcion Press, 1969.

Ratzinger, Joseph. "A Letter to the Bishops of the Roman Catholic Church on Some Aspects of Christian Meditation." *Origins* (Oct 15, 1989).

Samartha, Stanley. "The Progress and Promise of Interreligious Dialogue." *Journal of Ecumenical Studies* 9 no. 3 (1972): 463–476.

Schneiders, Sandra. "Spirituality in the Academy." *Theological Studies* 50 no. 4 (1989): 676–697.

————. "Theology and Spirituality: Strangers, Rivals, or Partners?" *Horizons* 13 no. 3 (1986): 253–274.

Simpson, T. "The New Dialogue between Christianity and Other Religions." *Theology* 92 (January 1989): 92–102.

Smith, Huston. "Is There a Perennial Philosophy?" *Journal of the American Academy of Religion* 55 (Fall 1987): 553–566.

Swearer, Donald. *A Theology of Dialogue.* Bangkok: Department of Christian Education and Literature, 1973.

Swindler, Leonard. "The Dialogue Decalogue: Ground Rules for Interreligious Dialogue." *Journal of Ecumenical Studies* 20 no. 1 (1983): 1–4.

————. "Interreligious Dialogue: A Christian Necessity." *Cross Currents* 35 nos. 2–3 (1985): 129–147.

————, ed. *Toward a Universal Theology of Religions.* Maryknoll, NY: Orbis, 1987.

Swindler, Leonard, and Seiichi Yagi. *A Bridge to Buddhist-Christian Dialogue.* New York: Paulist Press, 1990.

Tillich, Paul. *Christianity and the Encounter of the World Religions.* New York: Columbia University Press, 1963.

Thundy, Zacharias, et al., eds. *Religions in Dialogue: East and West Meet.* New York: University Press of America, 1985.

Toynbee, Arnold. *Christianity among the Religions of the World.* New York: Scribners, 1957.

Urubshurow, Victoria. "Love Is God: A Buddhist Interreligious Response to the Vatican Instruction on 'Some Aspects of Christian Meditation.'" *Buddhist-Christian Studies* 11 (1991): 151–172.

Vas, J. Clement. "Yoga and Christian Spirituality." *Spirituality Today* 33 no. 2 (1981): 150–158.

Vineeth, V. P. "Dialogue and Theology of Religious Pluralism: Theological Reflections." *Journal of Dharma* 14 no. 4 (1989): 376–396.

Vatican II, The Documents of. Boston: St Paul Editions, 1968.

Lumen Gentium (Constitution on the Church): 107–190.

Nostra Aetate (Relation to Non-Christian Religions): 253–260.

Dignitatis Humanae (Religious Liberty): 395–414.

Ad Gentes Divinus (Church's Missionary Activity): 459–512.

Gaudium et Spes (Church in the Modern World): 513–624.

Williams, George. "Understanding as the Goal of Some Historians of Religions." *Journal of Religious Thought* 27 no. 3 (1970): 50–61.

Williams, Paul. "Some Dimensions of the Recent Work of Raimundo Panikkar: A Buddhist Perspective." *Religious Studies* 27 no. 4 (1991): 511–521.

World Council of Churches. "The Baar Statement." Reprinted in *Buddhist Christian Studies* 11 (1991): 297–301.

Zaehner, R. C. *The Comparison of Religions.* Boston: Beacon Press, 1958.

Buddhist-Christian Dialogue

Abe, Maseo. "The Crucial Points: An Introduction to the Symposium on Christianity and Buddhism." *Japanese Religions* 8 no. 4 (1975): 2–9.

Appleton, George. *On the Eight-fold Path: Christian Practice Amida Buddhism.* New York: Oxford, 1961.

Balthasar, Hans Urs von. "Buddhism: An Approach to Dialogue." *Communio: International Catholic Review* 15 no. 4 (1988): 403–410.

———. "Christianity and Non-Christian Meditation." *Word and Spirit* 1 (1979): 147–166.

Barnard, L. W. "The Christian Approach to the East." *Theology* 61 (July 1958): 279–283.

Barnes, Michael. "Theological Trends: The Buddhist-Christian Dialogue." *The Way* 30 no. 1 (1990): 55–63.

Berthrong, John. "Trends in Contemporary Buddhist-Christian Dialogue." *Ecumenical Trends* 14 no. 9 (1985): 135–137.

Bragt, Jan van. "An East-West Spiritual Exchange." *Eastern Buddhist* 13 no. 1 (1980): 141–150.

Bruteau, Beatrice. "Global Spirituality and the Integration of East and West." *Cross Currents* 35 nos. 2–3 (1985): 190–205.

Buddhadasa, Bhikkhu. "Interfaith Understanding in the Buddhist-Christian Dialogue." *Buddhist-Christian Studies* 9 (1989): 233–235.

Cobb, John Jr. *Beyond Dialogue: Toward a Mutual Transformation of Christianity and Buddhism.* Philadelphia: Fortress Press, 1982.

Coff, Pascaline. "Eastern Influences on Benedictine Spirituality." *Cistercian Studies* 24 no. 3 (1989): 252–263.

------. "The Influence of Eastern Spiritual Traditions on the Contemplative Spirituality of Women in the Western Church." *Sisters Today* 51 no. 2 (1979): 73–78.

Conner, James. "Fifth Buddhist-Christian Meditation Conference at Naropa." *Journal of Ecumenical Studies* 22 no. 4 (1985): 880–881.

Coward, Harold. "The Possibility of Paradigm Choice in Buddhist-Christian Dialogue." *Journal of Ecumenical Studies* 25 no. 3 (1988): 370–382.

De Silva, Lynn. *The Problem of Self in Buddhism and Christianity.* Columbo: Ecumenical Institute for Study and Dialogue, 1984.

Dhavamony, Mariasusai, and Claude Geffre, eds. *Buddhism and Christianity.* New York: Crossroad, 1979.

Drummond, Richard. "Toward a Theological Understanding of Buddhism." *Journal of Ecumenical Studies* 7 no. 1 (1970): 1–22.

Fenton, John. "Buddhist Meditation and Christian Practice." *Anglican Theological Review* 53 no. 4 (1971): 237–251.

Fernando, Antony. *Buddhism and Christianity: Their Inner Affinity.* Columbo: Ecumenical Institute for Study and Dialogue, 1984.

------. "Salvation and Liberation in Buddhism and Christianity." *Lumen Vitae* 27 no. 2 (1972): 304–317.

Florida, Robert. "What Does Comparative Religion Compare: The Buddhist-Christian Example." *Studies in Religion/Sciences religieuses* 19 no. 2 (1990): 163–171.

Gardini, Walter. "Critical Points of the Buddhist-Christian Dialogue." *Japanese Religions* 9 no. 2 (1976): 33–46.

Hardy, Gilbert. "Eastern and Western Spirituality: At the Crossroads." *Communio: International Review* 10 no. 4 (1983): 360–377.

Ingram, Paul, and Frederick Streng, eds. *Buddhist Christian Dialogue: Mutual Renewal and Transformation.* Honolulu: University of Hawaii Press, 1986.

Johnston, William. *Christian Zen.* New York: Harper & Row, 1971.

King, Sallie. "Toward a Buddhist Model of Interreligious Dialogue." *Buddhist-Christian Studies* 9 (1989): 121–126.

King, Winston. "Buddhist-Christian Dialogue Reconsidered." *Buddhist-Christian Studies* 2 (1982): 5–11.

Knitter, Paul. "Horizons on Christianity's New Dialogue with Buddhism." *Horizons* 8 no. 1 (1981): 40–61.

————. "Spirituality and Liberation: A Buddhist-Christian Conversation." *Horizons* 15 no. 2 (1988): 347–364.

Leclerq, Jean. "Contemplation Revisited." *Buddhist-Christian Studies* 11 (1991): 285–288.

Lounsbery, G. Constant. *Buddhist Meditation in the Southern School: Theory and Practice for Westerner.* London: Luzac & Company LTD, 1950.

Loy, David. "A Zen Cloud? Comparing Zen Koan Practice with *The Cloud of Unknowing.*" *Buddhist Christian Studies* 9 (1989): 43–60.

Marquette, Jacques. *Introduction to Comparative Mysticism.* Bombay: Bharatiya Vidya Bhavan, 1965.

Meadow, Mary Jo. *Gentling the Heart: Buddhist Loving-kindness Practice for Christians.* New York: Crossroad, 1994.

Meadow, Mary Jo, et al. *Purifying the Heart: Buddhist Insight Meditation for Christians.* New York: Crossroad, 1994.

Merton, Thomas. *The Asian Journal.* New York: New Directions, 1973.

————. *Mystics and Zen Masters.* New York: Dell Publishing, 1967.

————. *Zen and the Birds of Appetite.* New York: New Directions, 1968.

Mitchell, Donald. "The Place of the Self in Christian Spirituality: A Response to the Buddhist-Christian Dialogue." *Japanese Religions* 13 no. 3 (1984): 2–26.

————. *Spirituality and Emptiness: The Dynamics of Spiritual Life in Buddhism and Christianity.* New York: Paulist Press, 1991.

Moomaers, Paul, and Jan Van Bragt. *Mysticism: Buddhist and Christian.* New York: Paulist Press, 1995.

Morris, Augustine. "Buddhist-Christian Monastic Contemplative Encounter." *Buddhist-Christian Studies* 9 (1989): 247–255.

Nakamura, Hajime. *Buddhism in Comparative Light.* New Delhi: Islam and the Modern Age Society, 1975.

O'Hanlon, Danniel. "Enroute to Asia: Seeking Essentials to Religious Reality." *National Catholic Reporter* 11 (July 18, 1975): 7–8.

Pennington, Basil. "Looking East—Seeing West." *America* 134 no. 9 (1976): 180–182.

Pfister, Lauren. "Reconsidering the Grounds for Buddhist-Christian Dialogic Communication: A Review of John D'Arcy May's *Meaning, Consensus and Dialogue in Buddhist-Christian Communion.*" *Buddhist-Christian Studies* 6 (1986): 121–138.

Pieris, Aloysius. "Christianity and Buddhism in Core-to-Core Dialogue." *Cross Currents* 37 no. 1 (1975): 47–75.

———. *Love Meets Wisdom: A Christian Experience of Buddhism.* Maryknoll, NY: Orbis, 1988.

Reat, N. Ross. "Buddhist-Christian Dialogue: Whether, Whence and Why." In *Perspectives on Language and Text,* ed. E. Conrad and E. Newing, pp. 425–432. Winona Lake, IN: Eisenbrauns, 1987.

Riesenhuber, Klaus. "Understanding Non-objective Meditation." *Communio: International Catholic Review* 15 no. 4 (1988): 451–467.

Scheuer, Jacques. "Buddhists and Christians: Towards a Closer Encounter." *Lumen Vitae* 39 no. 1 (1984): 11–27.

Seifert, Friedrich. "Historical-Critical Analysis and Buddhist-Christian Dialogue." *Buddhist-Christian Studies* 2 (1982): 63–77.

Steindl-Rast, David. "A Shift in Buddhist-Christian Dialogue." *Aereapogus* 2 no. 1 (1988): 18–20.

Swindler, Leonard, and Seiichi Yagi. *A Bridge to Buddhist-Christian Dialogue.* New York: Paulist Press, 1990.

Teasdale, Wayne. "The Nature of *Sannyasa* and Its Value for Christian Spirituality." *Communio: International Catholic Review* 12 no. 3 (1985): 325–334.

Waldenfels, Hans. "Buddhism and Christianity in Dialogue: Notes on the Intellectual Presuppositions." *Communio: International Catholic Review* 15 no. 4 (1988): 411–422.

Walker, Susan, ed. *Speaking of Silence: Christians and Buddhists on the Contemplative Way.* New York: Paulist Press, 1987.

Wells, Harry Lee. *The Problem of the Phenomenal Self: A Study of the Buddhist Doctrine of Anatta with Specific Regard to Buddhist-Christian Dialogue.* PhD Diss. Ann Arbor, MI: UMI, 1988.

Wilfred, Felix. "Asia and Western Christianity." *Pacifica* 2 no. 3 (1989): 268–281.

Saint John of the Cross

Primary Texts

John of the Cross, Saint. *The Collected Works of St. John of the Cross* (rev.). Trans. and ed. Kavanaugh and Rodriquez. Washington, DC: ICS, 1991.

San Juan de la Cruz. *Obras Completas* [2 vols.]. Edicion de Luce Lopez-Baralt y Eulogio Pacho. Madrid: Alianza Editorial, 1991.

Secondary Texts

Bechtle, Regina. "Theological Trends: Convergences in Theology and Spirituality." *The Way* 25 (Fall 1985): 305–314.

Bendick, Johannes. "God and the Word in St. John of the Cross." *Philosophy Today* 16 (Winter 1972): 281–294.

Boulet, Jean. *"Nier Dieu pour le connaître."* Foi et vie 77 (S 1978): 17–30.

Bouyer, Louis. *Introduction to Spirituality.* New York: Desclee, 1961.

Bouyer, Louis, et al., ed. Boyer. *A History of Christian Spirituality* [4 vols.]. Trans. Mary Ryan. New York: Seabury Press, 1963.

Brenan, Gerald. *St. John of the Cross: His Life and Poetry.* London: Cambridge University Press, 1973.

Burrows, Ruth. *Ascent to Love: The Spiritual Teaching of St. John of the Cross.* London: Darton, Longman and Todd, 1987.

Buruzi, Jean. *"San Juan de la Cruz y el problema de la experiencia mística."* Revisita augustiniana 33 (Fall 1992): 1188–1490.

Cadrecha, M. *"San Juan de la Cruz: Una eclesiologie de amor."* Salmanticensis 32 (Fall 1985): 401–403.

Carmody, John Tully. "The Contemporary Significance of *no se que.*" *Spiritual Life* 37 (Spring 1991): 30–37.

Coelho, Mary. "Understanding Consolation and Desolation." *Review for Religious* 44 (Jan–Feb 1985): 61–77.

Collings, Ross. *John of the Cross.* Collegeville: Liturgical Press, 1990.

Crisógono, de Jesús. *The Life of St. John of the Cross.* Trans. Kathleen Pond. London: Longmans, 1958.

Cugno, Alain. *St. John of the Cross: Reflections on Mystical Experiences.* Trans. Barbara Wall. New York: Seabury Press, 1982.

Culligan, Kevin. "John of the Cross: A Personality Profile." *Spiritual Life* 37 (Winter 1991): 198–211.

———. "Mysticism, Transformation and Spiritual Discipline: The Teachings of St. John of the Cross." *Spiritual Life* 30 (Fall 1984): 131–142.

———. "Pastoral Minister as Ardent Lover: Saint John of the Cross's Challenge for the American Church," an unpublished lecture given at the symposium, "John of the Cross—A Resource for Pastoral Ministry Today." Holy Hill—Shrine of Mary Help of Christians (Hubertus, WI, December 14–15, 1990).

———. "Saint John of the Cross and Modern Psychology." *Studies in Formative Spirituality* 13 (Fall 1992): 29–48.

Daggy, Robert. "Thomas Merton's Practical Norms of Sanctity in St. John of the Cross." *Spiritual Life* 36 (Winter 1990): 195–201.

Dent, Barbara. "Leaping into the Abyss." *Spiritual Life* 35 (Spring 1989): 35–47.

Dicken, Truman. *The Crucible of Love: A Study of the Mysticism of St. Teresa of Jesus and St. John of the Cross.* New York: Sheed & Ward, 1963.

Dodd, Michael. "Beginners and the Spiritual Canticle: A Reflection." *Spiritual Life* 29 (Winter 1983): 195–208.

———. "St. John of the Cross and Friendship." *Spiritual Life* 26 (Winter 1980): 194–204.

Dubay, Thomas. *Fire Within.* San Francisco: Ignatius Press, 1989.

Duque, Jimenez. *En torno a San Juan de la Cruz.* Barcelona: Juan Flor, 1960.

Edwards, James Denis. *The Dynamism in Faith: The Interaction between Experience of God and Explicit Faith: A Comparative Study of the Mystical Theology of John of the Cross and the Transcendental Theology of Karl Rahner.* PhD Diss. Ann Arbor, MI: UMI, 1979.

Eileen, Sister Mary. *Pilgrimage and Possession: Conversion in the Writings of St. John of The Cross.* Oxford: SLG, 1987.

Ellis, Robert. *San Juan de la Cruz: Mysticism and Sartrean Existentialism.* New York: Peter Lang, 1992.

Galielea, Segundo. "St. John of the Cross and Spirituality in America." *Spiritual Life* 35 (Summer 1989): 67–78.

Garcia, Ciro. *"Juan de la Cruz y el misterio del hombre."* *Salmanticensis* 38 (Winter 1991): 99–100.

Gaudreau, Marie. *Mysticism and Image in St. John of the Cross.* Bern: Herbert Lang, 1976.

Giallanza, Joel. "Myths of Detachment." *Spiritual Life* 27 (Winter 1981): 210–218.

———. "Responding to Our World in Faith." *Living Prayer* 24 (January 1991): 3–9.

Gilbert, Paul. *"Une anthropologie à partir de Saint Jean de la Croix; à propos d'un ouvrage récent."* *Nouvelle revue theologique* 103 (Jl–Aug 1981): 551–562.

Goeldt, Michael de. *"L'aspiration de l'Espirit Saint au coeur de l'home selon Jean de la Croix."* *Lumiere* 34 (Jl–S 1985): 49–63.

Griffin, Michael. "The Ladder of Love in St. John of the Cross." *Spiritual Life* 29 (Spring 1983): 2–9.

Hardy, Richard. "Fidelity to God in the Mystical Experience of *Fray Juan de la Cruz.*" *Eglise et théologie* 11 (January 1980): 57–75.

———. *Search for Nothing: The Life of St. John of the Cross.* New York: Crossroad, 1982.

———. *"Silencio divino:* A Sanjuanist Study." *Eglise et théologie* 7 (May 1976): 219–233.

Holotik, Gerhard. *"Les sources de la spiritualite Catholique selon Vat. II."* *Nouvelle revue theologique* 109 (Ja–F 1987): 66–77.

Hovley, Vincent. *Love in St. John of the Cross: A Contribution to Spiritual Theology.* PhD Diss. Ann Arbor, MI: UMI, 1978.

Jatzen, Grace. "A Language of Desire." *The Way* 30 (January 1990): 26–36.

Jennings, Elizabeth. "Innocent Audacity: An Approach to St. John of the Cross." *Blackfriars* 42 (Fall 1961): 60–69.

Johnston, William. "All and Nothing: St. John of the Cross and the Christian-Buddhist Dialogue." *Eastern Buddhist* 21 (Fall 1988): 124–144.

Kane, Thomas. *Gentleness in John of the Cross.* Oxford: SLG Press, 1985.

Kavanaugh, Kieran. "The Death of God and St. John of the Cross." *Spiritual Life* 12 (Winter 1966): 260–269.

———. "The Garden." *Living Prayer* 24 (May 1991): 8–12.

———. "St. John of the Cross: On Aridity and Contemplation." *Spiritual Life* 8 (Fall 1962): 182–193.

Keller, Joseph. "The Function of Paradox in Mystical Discourse." *Studia Mystica* 6 (Fall 1983): 3–19.

Kerr, Susan. "The Inner Monastery." *Spiritual Life* 34 (Summer 1988): 73–74.

Kloepfer, John. "Spiritual Development and the Disposition of Openness." *Studies in Formative Spirituality* 13 (Winter 1991): 87–102.

Kristo, Jure. "The Interpretation of Religious Experience: What Do Mystics Intend When They Talk about their Experience?" *Journal of Religion* 62 (January 1982): 21–30.

Lallement, Lois. *La Voie de l'Espirit: L'adventure intérieur et le plein accomplissment de l'homme selon de maîtres spirituels et le témoignage de mystique.* Paris: Beauchesne, 1981.

Laux, Henri. *"L'Expérience de negation chez Saint Jean de la Croix."* *Recherches de science religieuse* 10 (Ap–Je 1992): 203–226.

Le Blond, Jean-Marie. *"Le sens de l'existence humaine."* *Etudes* 307 (Winter 1960): 411–414.

Lefebvre, Dom Georges. *"Les purifications de la prière d'apres Saint Jean de la Croix."* *Vie spirituelle* 101 (November 1959): 392–412.

Lechner, Robert. "St. John of the Cross and Sacramental Experience." *Worship* 34 (October 1960): 544–551.

Leonard, Linda. "Toward an Ontological Analysis of Detachment." *Philosophy Today* 16 (Winter 1972): 268–280.

Loebig, Mary Jo. "Seeking the Hidden Face of God." *Living Prayer* 23 (January 1990): 21–23.

Lund, Leslie. "Desire in St. John of the Cross." *Spiritual Life* 31 (Summer 1985): 83–100.

Maio, Eugene. *St. John of the Cross: The Imagery of Eros.* Madrid: Collecion Plaza Mayor Scholar, 1973.

Mather, J. "Detachment in the Ascent of Mt. Carmel: An Appreciation." *Review for Religious* 38 (Spring 1979): 641–649.

McInnis, Judy. "Eucharistic and Conjugal Symbolism in the Spiritual Canticle of St. John of the Cross." *Renascence* 36 (Spring 1884): 118–136.

McMahon, John. *The Divine Union in the Subida Del Monte Carmelo and the Nocha Oscura of St. John of the Cross.* PhD Diss. Washington, DC: Catholic University of America Press, 1941.

Millette, Edele. "The Third Dark Night." *Contemplative Review* 18 (Fall 1985): 14–17.

Milos, Joy. "Traditions of Spiritual Guidance: Evelyn Underhill, A Companion on Many Journeys." *The Way* 30 (April 1990): 147–157.

Moreno, Antonio. "Contemplation According to Teresa and John of the Cross." *Review for Religious* 37 (March 1978): 256–267.

Muto, Susan. "The Counsels of John of the Cross: Wisdom for Today." *Spiritual Life* 37 (Winter 1991): 212–224.

———. "The First Stage to Union: The Active Night of the Senses." *Review for Religious* 46 (Mar–Apr 1987): 161–177.

———. "The Hunger, the Thirst for Wholeness, for Holiness." *Envoy* 20 (Nov–Dec 1983): 12–13.

———. "Light and Darkness." *Living Prayer* 24 (May 1991): 20–24.

Navone, John. "The Graves of Craving and Self-Fulfillment." *Homiletic and Pastoral Review* 81 (November 1980): 29–32; 52–54.

O'Donoghue, Noel. *Mystics for Our Time: Carmelite Meditations for a New Age.* Edinburgh: T & T Clark, 1989.

Oliver, Leroy. *"Quelques traits de Saint Jean de la Croix comme maître spirituel."* Carmelus 11 (1964): 3–43.

Payne, Steven. "The Christian Character of Christian Mystical Experiences." *Religious Studies* 20 (S 1984): 417–427.

———. *St. John of the Cross and the Cognitive Value of Mysticism: An Analysis of Sanjuanist Teaching and Its Philosophical Implications for Contemporary Discussions of Mystical Experience.* Boston: Kluwer Academic Publishers, 1990.

———, ed. *Carmelite Studies, VI.* Washington, DC: ICS, 1992.

Payne, Steven, and Michael Dodd. "Master in Faith: John of the Cross for Today." *Listening* 26 (Fall 1991): 232–245.

Peers, Edgar Allison. *Spirit of Flame: A Study of St. John of the Cross.* New York: Morehouse & Gorham, 1944.

———, ed. *Councils of Light and Love.* New York: Paulist Press, 1987.

Richard, R. *"La tradition dionysienne en Espange après Saint Jean de la Croix."* Revue d'ascetique et mystic 45 (1969): 419–424.

Rodriguez-San, Pedro, and Luis Enrique. *"San Juan de la Cruz en la Universidad de Salamanca* 1564–1568." *Salmanticensis* 36 (Summer 1989): 157–192.

Ruiz, Frederico, et al. *God Speaks in the Night: The Life, Times, and Teachings of St. John of the Cross.* Trans. K. Kavavaugh. Washington, DC: ICS Publications, 1991.

Russell, Paul. "The Humanity of Christ in St. John of the Cross." *Spiritual Life* 30 (Winter 1984): 143–156.

Saint Joseph, Lucien-Marie de. *"Un Guide de lecture pour Saint Jean de la Croix."* *Vie spirituelle* 101 (November 1959): 413–423.

———. *Actualité de Jean de la Croix: recueil des études présentées au Congrès de la Plesse, Angers, 1968.* Brussels: Desclée de Brouwer, 1970.

Sanderlin, David. "Charity according to Saint John of the Cross: A Distinguished Love for Interesting Special Relationships, including Marriage." *Journal of Religious Ethics* 27 (Spring 1993): 87–115.

Steggint, Otger, ed. *Juan de la Cruz: Espíritu de Llama.* Kampen, The Netherlands: Kok Pharos Publishing House, 1991.

Thompson, Colin. *The Poet and Mystic: A Study of the Cantico Espiritual of San Juan de la Cruz.* New York: Oxford University Press, 1977.

Toft, Evelyn. *San Juan de la Cruz: A New Perspective on Contemplation.* PhD Diss., University of Cincinnati, 1983.

———. "Some Contexts for the Ascetical Language of John of the Cross." *Mystics Quarterly* 17 (March 1991): 27–35.

Tohurst, James. "In Darkness and Secure: The Wisdom of St. John of the Cross." *Priest and People* 21 (March 1989): 97–100.

Tugwell, Simon. "Spirituality and Negative Spirituality." *New Blackfriars* 68 (May 1987): 257–263.

Turner, Denys. "St. John of the Cross and Depression." *Downside Review* 106 (July 1988): 157–170.

Van Eck, Petra, and Frank England. "The Way of Dispossession: Modern Theology Engages with a Saint." *Journal of Theology for Southern Africa* 73 (December 1990): 60–66.

Virant, Vera Lea. "Voices out of Crisis." *Spiritual Life* 27 (Fall 1981): 167–177.

Welch, John. *When Gods Die: An Introduction to St. John of the Cross.* New York: Paulist Press, 1990.

Wilhelmsen, Elizabeth. *Cognition and Communication in John of the Cross.* New York: P. Lang, 1985.

Williams, Dan. "The Poet–Contemplative Dilemma." *Spiritual Life* 24 (Spring 1978): 18–24.

Theravada Buddhism

Primary Texts

Buddhaghosa, Bhadantacariya. *Visuddhimagga.* Rev. Dharmananda Kosambi and ed. Henri Clark Warren. Delhi: Motilal Banarsadass, 1950.

———. *The Path of Purification (Visuddhimagga).* Trans. Nanamoli. Kandy: Buddhist Publication Society, 1991.

Secondary Texts

Adikarem, E. W. *The Early History of Buddhism in Ceylon.* Dehiwala, Sri Lanka: Buddhist Cultural Centre, 1946.

Bond, George. "The Arahant: *Sainthood in Theravada Buddhism.*" In *Sainthood: Its Manifestations in World Religions.* Kieckhefer and Bond, eds. Berkeley: University of California Press, 1988, pp. 140–171.

Buswell, Robert E. Jr., and Robert M. Gimello, eds. *Paths to Liberation: The Marga and Its Transformations in Buddhist Thought.* Honolulu: University of Hawaii Press, 1992.

Carter, John. "Compassion as Given in Christianity and Theravada Buddhism." *Eastern Buddhist* 22 (Spring 1989): 27–53.

———. "History of Early Buddhism." *Religious Studies* 13 (Spring 1977): 263–287.

Collins, Steven. *Selfless Persons: Imagery and Thought in Theravada Buddhism.* Cambridge: Cambridge University Press, 1982.

Conze, Edward. *Buddhist Texts through the Ages.* San Francisco: Harper-Collins, 1964.

Davids, Rhys, ed. *Compendium of Philosophy (Abhidhammattha-Sangaha).* London: Pali Text Society, 1956.

Donnet, Daniel, ed. *Indianisme et Bouddhisme: Mélanges offerts à Mgr Étienne Lamotte.* Louvain-la-Neuve: Université Catholique de Louvain, 1980.

Dumoulin, Heinrich, ed. *Buddhism in the Modern World.* New York: Macmillan Publishing, 1976.

Edwards, Felicite. "Vipassana Meditation and Transcultural Consciousness." *Journal for the Study of Religion* 1 (Spring 1988): 37–51.

Goldstein, Joseph. *The Experience of Insight: A Simple and Direct Guide to Buddhist Meditation.* Boston: Shambhala, 1987.

———. *Insight Meditation: The Practice of Freedom.* Boston: Shambala, 1994.

———. *Transforming the Mind, Healing the World.* New York: Paulist Press, 1994.

Goldstein, Joseph, and Jack Kornfield. Seeking the Heart of Wisdom: *The Path of Insight Meditation.* Boston: Shambhala, 1987.

Gombrich, Richard. *Theravada Buddhism: A Social History from Benares to Modern Columbo.* London: Routledge, 1988.

Griffiths, Paul. "Concentration or Insight: The Problematic of Theravada Buddhism." *Journal of the American Academy of Religion* 49 (December 1981): 605–624.

———. *On Being Mindless: Buddhist Meditation and the Mind-Body Problem.* La Salle, IL: Open Court, 1986.

Gunarantana, Henepola. *Mindfulness in Plain English.* Boston: Wisdom Publications, 1991.

———. *The Path of Serenity and Insight: An Explanation of Buddhist Jhanas.* Delhi: Motilal Benarsidass, 1985.

Johansson, Rune. *The Psychology of Nirvana.* London: Allen & Unwin, 1969.

Kalupahana, David. *Buddhist Philosophy: An Historical Analysis.* Honolulu: University Press of Hawaii, 1976.

———. *The Principles of Buddhist Psychology.* Albany: State University of New York Press, 1987.

Kaviratna, Harischandra, trans. and ed. *Dhammapada: Wisdom of the Buddha.* Pasadena, CA: Theosophical University Press, 1980.

Kema, Ayya. "Twelve Conditions Leading to Nibbana." *Middle Way* 65 (Aug–Nov 1990): 83–88; 149–155.

Khantipalo, Bhikkhu. *Calm and Insight: A Buddhist Manual for Meditators.* London: Curxon Press, 1981.

King, Winston. "Sacramental Aspects of Theravada Buddhist Meditation." *Numen* 36 (December 1989): 248–256.

———. "Structure and Dynamics of Attainment of Cessation in Theravada Meditation." *Journal of the American Academy of Religion* 45 (1977): 707–725.

———. *Theravada Meditation: The Buddhist Transformation of Yoga.* University Park: Pennsylvania State University Press, 1980.

Kornfield, Jack. *Living Buddhist Masters.* Kandy: Buddhist Publication Society, 1977.

Kornfield, Jack, and Paul Breiter, eds. *A Still Forest Pool: Insight Meditation of Achaan Chah.* Wheaton, IL: Theosophical Publishing House, 1985.

Krishan, Y. "Buddhism and Belief in *Atma.*" *Journal of the International Association of Buddhist Studies* 7 no. 2 (1984): 117–135.

Law, Bimala Charan. *The Life and Work of Buddhaghosa.* Delhi: Nag Publishers, 1976.

Lester, Robert. *Theravada Buddhism in Southeast Asia.* Ann Arbor: University of Michigan Press, 1973.

Masefield, Peter. "The Nibbana-Parinibbana Controversy." *Religion* 9 (Fall 1979): 215–230.

Mitchell, Donald. "Analysis in Theravada Buddhism." *Philosophy East and West* 21 no. 1 (1971): 23–31.

Nanamoli, Bhikkhu and Bhikkhu Bodhi, trans. *The Middle Length Discourses of the Buddha [Majjhima Nikaya].* Boston: Wisdom Publications, 1995.

Nyanaponika, Thera. *The Heart of Buddhist Meditation.* York Beach, ME: Samuel Weiser, Inc., 1965.

———. *The Vision of Dhamma.* London: Rider, 1986.

———, ed. *Pathways of Buddhist Thought: Essays from the Wheel.* London: Allen & Unwin, 1971.

Nyanatiloka, Thera. *Path to Deliverance.* Colombo: Bauddha Sahitya Sahbha, 1952.

Palihawadana, Mahinda. "Is There a Theravada Buddhist Idea of Grace?" *Dialogue (Colombo)* 9 nos. 1–3 (1982): 91–103.

Panikkar, Raimundo. *The Silence of God: An Answer of the Buddha.* Trans. Robert Barr. Maryknoll, NY: Orbis, 1989.

Peret, Edmond. *"Voies de contemplation dans Bouddisme Theravada,"* in *Meditation dans le Christianisme et les autres religions,* ed M. Dhavamony et al., p. 67. Rome: Gregorian University Press, 1976.

Sayadaw, Mahasi. *The Progress of Insight through the Stages of Purification.* Trans. Nyanaponika Thera. Kandy: Forest Hermitage Press, 1965.

———. *The Satipatthana Vipassana Meditation.* Trans. U Pe Thin. San Francisco: Unity Press, 1971.

Shaftel, Oscar. *Understanding the Buddha.* New York: Schoeken Books, 1974.

Silananda, U. *The Four Foundations of Mindfulness.* Boston: Wisdom Publications, 1990.

Soma, Thera. *The Way of Mindfulness: The Satipattana Sutta and Commentary.* Kandy: Buddhist Publication Society, 1975.

Spiro, Melford. *Buddhism and Society,* 2nd ed. Berkeley: University of California Press, 1982.

Tin, Pe Maung. *Buddhist Devotion and Meditation: An Objective Description and Study.* London: S.P.C.K., 1964.

U Pandita, Sayadaw. *In This Very Life: The Liberation Teachings of the Buddha.* Trans. U Aggacitta. Boston: Wisdom Publications, 1991.

Vajiranana, Pravahera. *Buddhist Meditation in Theory and Practice.* Kuala Lumpur, Malaysia: Buddhist Missionary Society, 1962.

———. *"Paramita* (The Perfections)." *Middle Way* 65 (Aug–Nov 1990): 67–70; 131–133.

Walsh, Maurice, trans. and ed. *Thus Have I Heard: The Long Discourses of the Buddha [Digha Nikaya].* London: Wisdom Publications, 1987.

Waters, John. *Mind Unshaken: A Modern Approach to Buddhism.* London: Rider & Company, 1961.

Wells, Harry Lee. *The Problem with the Phenomenal Self: A Study of the Buddhist Doctrine of Anatta with Specific Regard to Buddhist-Christian Dialogue.* PhD Diss. Southern Baptist Theological Seminary, 1988.

Wijayaratna, Mohan. *Buddhist Monastic Life According to the Texts of the Theravada Tradition.* Trans. Grangier and Collins. Cambridge: Cambridge University Press, 1990.

Yoshinori, Takeuchi. *The Heart of Buddhism: In Search of the Timeless Spirit of Primitive Buddhism.* Trans. and ed. James Heisig. New York: Crossroad, 1983.

Index (with Buddhist terms translated)

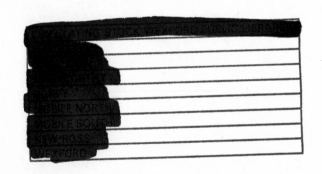
LAST IN CIRC.
18/12/17